How to Lead, Adapt, and Win in an AI-Driven World

LEADING IN THE NEW RETIREMENT ERA

Carroll S. Golden

First Printing 2025

Book Design and Interior by Best Holistic Life Publishing

Manufactured in the United States of America

2025918392

Library of Congress Cataloging-in-Publication Data

Names: Golden, Carroll S., author
Title: Leading In The New Retirement Era: How to Lead, Adapt, and Win in an AI-Driven World/ Carroll S. Golden
Identifiers: LCCN 2025918392 | ISBN 9789699092633 (hardcover) | ISBN 9789699092626 (paperback) | ISBN 9789699092640 (ebook) | ISBN 9789699092657 (audio)
Subjects: Financial Health | Self-Growth | Self-Help| Financial Growth & Legacy

ISBN 978-969-9092-63-3 (hardcover)
ISBN 978-969-9092-62-6 (paperback)
ISBN 978-969-9092-64-0 (ebook)
ISBN 978-969-9092-65-7 (audio)

Acknowledgments

Writing a book is a lot like assembling furniture without the instructions—messy, confusing, and full of unexpected hardware. Thankfully, I didn't have to do it alone.

First, my deepest thanks to my publisher, Jana Short, and her amazing team. You turned what could have been a stressful process into a smooth (and even fun) journey. Your dedication and support kept this book moving forward even on the days I couldn't.

To my friends and peers at the National Association of Insurance and Financial Advisors—you're more than colleagues. You're the kind of people who show up, lift others, and remind me why this work matters. You've been cheering me on before I even had a title for this thing.

A very special nod to Dan Mangus, who always says yes to "Can I run this by you?" and somehow turns every conversation into something sharper and stronger. Your willingness to think out loud with me—repeatedly—helped this book find its voice.

And finally, to Ernesto Verdugo. Thank you for pushing me past the edges of my comfort zone and into something bold, clear, and bigger than I imagined. Thank you for showing me that "beyond the ordinary AI" is not only possible, it's the only place worth going.

Preface

I didn't set out to write a book on retirement. In fact, I thought I had that part of my life—and my planning—figured out. But somewhere between reviewing my own retirement plan and talking with my very capable financial professional, it hit me: we were both staring at a roadmap that no longer matched the terrain.

That realization was the spark.

Over time, I noticed that many financial professionals were running into the same problem. They *knew* the world of retirement was shifting. They saw how their clients were living longer, retiring differently, and asking deeper questions. But many of them were just too busy, too swamped, or too unsure of where to begin shifting their own approach.

So, I wrote this to offer a starting place. Or, more accurately, four.

Whether you're new to the profession, stuck somewhere between transactional and truly transitional planning, or considering your own exit with client concerns still top of mind, this book is meant to offer a fresh approach. You'll find four distinct paths inside—not rules, but routes. Choose one. Or blend them. The point is: there isn't just *one* way forward anymore.

My hope is that you walk away from this book with ideas that feel like yours. Maybe a renewed sense of purpose. Maybe a little validation. Maybe a reminder that your work doesn't just matter—it echoes through generations. If not—well, at least the chapters are short and there's no quiz at the end.

Thanks for picking this up. Now let's walk this road together.

—Carroll

Foreword

"I've had the privilege of working in financial planning for many years, and while the foundation of our work remains timeless, the expectations and needs of our clients are anything but static. Today's clients face challenges we couldn't have anticipated just a decade ago—from the ever-increasing costs of healthcare to the desire for a more meaningful legacy. Carroll's book, written by an expert who truly understands the future of retirement and financial planning, provides a roadmap for advisors ready to embrace this evolution.

Her books provide invaluable insights into healthcare planning, each one a testament to her practical expertise and dedication to the field. Over the years, she has honed her mastery of the subject, offering guidance that resonates with both clarity and purpose. Collaborating with Carroll is more than a professional alliance—it is a pathway to transforming your role from a conventional advisor to a trusted coordinator within the family's support network. This shift not only enhances your immediate impact but also establishes a legacy, fostering relationships that extend across generations. By adopting the approach outlined here, we don't just help clients build wealth; we empower them to navigate life's most significant transitions with confidence. I invite every advisor who reads these pages to lean into this forward-thinking model—it's not only the future of financial planning, but also a way to leave an indelible mark on those we serve."

Barbara Pietrangleo, CFP, CLU, ChFC, LUTCF, RFC, CLTC
Certified Financial Planner,
Past Board chair of Life Happens,
NAIFA Trustee,
Past president of the MDRT Foundation
In the industry for over 30 years

Dedication

For Nicole and Erik, who are my why.
And for those who've walked beside me in growth, transition, and belief—thank you for making the leap matter- this book carries your fingerprints.

Disclaimer

Neither the author nor the other contributors offer this information as tax, legal, investment, retirement advice, or recommendations. The content is derived from sources believed to be accurate. Neither the information presented nor any opinion expressed constitutes a solicitation for the purchase or sale of any product or security. The interpretation of planning tools and products is used in the context of the story but may also be applicable to other planning situations. Please consult an agent, investment advisor, tax consultant, or attorney before making a tax-related investment/insurance decision.

Table of Contents

INTRODUCTION

The Advisor's Dilemma: Leading the Charge in the New Retirement Era

The financial advisory profession stands at a crossroads. The traditional playbook, centered on wealth accumulation and market performance, no longer suffices. A fundamental shift is underway, one that demands **leadership, innovation, and an unwavering commitment to meeting clients where they truly are.**

A recent study by OneAmerica Financial and another by Lincoln Financial revealed a startling reality: nearly every financial advisor has encountered clients facing the need for extended or long-term care. This contingency can double a client's portfolio withdrawal rate when uninsured or unprepared. This shift demands a recalibration of priorities, as rising medical and extended care costs eclipse traditional concerns like inflation or market volatility. Financial advisors must move beyond viewing these issues as secondary. Yet many advisors hesitate. They avoid difficult conversations. They assume clients will figure it out on their own or that insurance agents will step in. They rely on outdated models that fail to account for the three essential stages of retirement—pre-Medicare, Medicare, and post-Medicare, or the go-go, slow-go, and no-go years as they have been labeled. As a result, they risk losing not just assets under management, but also the very trust and credibility that define their profession.

A New Era Opportunity: Go Beyond Numbers

The challenge extends far beyond balance sheets and withdrawal strategies. Advisors today face an escalating crisis of client attrition—not because of fees or returns, but because of unmet expectations, impersonal service, and a failure to demonstrate value beyond investments. Clients don't just want a financial planner; they want a guide—someone who understands their fears, their family dynamics, and their evolving needs.

A Morningstar Behavioral Research study confirms what the industry has been sensing: an advisor's value is no longer defined by performance alone, but by their ability to provide clarity, confidence, and a roadmap for life's transitions.

When advisors only *tell* clients what they can do instead of *showing them* how to navigate longevity, health challenges, and financial security, they sow the seeds of doubt. In today's hyper-connected world, that doubt doesn't linger—it drives clients straight into the arms of another firm.

A New Era Reality: The $68-84 Trillion Wealth Transfer

This industry shift isn't just a challenge—it's the biggest opportunity financial professionals have seen in decades. Over the next 25 years, somewhere between $68 and $84 trillion will change hands as Baby Boomers pass their wealth to Gen X, Millennials, and Gen Z. This isn't a prediction; it's already in motion. According to updated projections from

Cerulli Associates, the total transfer could reach $124 trillion by 2048, with $105 trillion going to heirs and $18 trillion to charitable causes.

This "Great Wealth Transfer" isn't just about money—it's about relationships, trust, and a complete shift in expectations. The next generation of clients won't just inherit assets—they'll inherit decisions, responsibilities, and a completely different view of what financial advice should look like. They expect clarity, technology that works for them, and a personal connection that goes beyond performance reports.

For financial professionals, this is the time to step forward—not just to retain assets, but to serve as a steady hand through one of the most meaningful transitions in modern financial history. The Great Wealth Transfer isn't simply about numbers. It's about people, legacy, and life-changing choices. As Baby Boomers pass the torch, financial professionals have both an opportunity and an ethical duty: to guide families, protect values, and help new generations understand what wealth can and cannot really do.

These days, anyone can run the numbers with an app—but understanding what those numbers mean, and how they align with someone's goals, values, and fears? And experience isn't just about age—it's about perspective. A skilled advisor understands that each generation brings its own lens, shaped by different challenges, beliefs, and ambitions.

This moment demands more than planning—it demands purpose. The Great Wealth Transfer isn't just about moving money from one generation to the next; it's about passing along values, intentions, and deeply personal goals. Each client brings a different story and a different vision for the future. Some want to grow their legacy. Others hope to give much of it away. Many simply want to know that, in the long run, they'll be able to support the people they care about or simply live life on their terms. In times like these, the role of the financial professional isn't just to build a plan—it's to help clients make sense of what their wealth truly means.

That's where the true impact of a great advisor shines. It's not just about managing money—it's about managing meaning, helping one generation honor their hard work while preparing the next to carry it forward and being the bridge between spreadsheets and dreams, between risk assessments and real-life priorities.

Financial professionals have the opportunity to emerge as trusted voices during this transition, offering a nuanced understanding of what truly matters and to whom it matters. And that's what builds lifelong loyalty—not just from one client, but from an entire family.

A New Era Tool: AI is Here

AI isn't just a tool anymore—it's becoming a team member. In the financial world, this means it can handle repetitive number-crunching, allowing professionals to focus on what matters most: people. In financial services and planning, time isn't just money—it's opportunity, reputation, and results. Every minute spent buried in paperwork or juggling back-end processes is a minute not spent helping clients navigate their future. Whether it's building retirement plans, managing investments, or guiding someone through a major life change, your time directly impacts their trust and your bottom line.

Clients don't just pay for advice—they pay for attention. They want your insights, your strategy, and your presence. This is where smart automation steps in. AI and digital tools aren't here to replace the advisor—they're here to give them back part of their day. By clearing the clutter and repetitive time-consuming tasks, professionals can redirect their energy toward research, client and professional relationships, in-depth planning, and informed decision-making.

The truth is that your calendar is your most *valuable asset.* When you protect it with efficient systems and technology that work behind the scenes, you're not just saving time—you're making room for stronger outcomes and generating more satisfied and loyal clients over time.

But AI isn't just about speed or data. It's about connection. Imagine a client getting an update that sounds flat and robotic—it feels cold, even if the numbers are right. That's why more firms are adding personality to their AI tools. They're building systems that not only work smart, but also talk smart.

Think of it this way: your AI should sound like your firm. If your message is scrambled, so will the resulting message produced by AI. Whether that's calm and professional or warm and friendly, clients notice when a message feels human. This personal touch fosters trust, maintains clear communication, and helps clients feel more at ease when asking questions or making decisions.

Some firms are going further—teaching their AI to reflect company values, explain financial topics in plain English, and even match the tone of each advisor. It turns everyday updates into real conversations and helps clients feel like they're dealing with people, not just programs. For financial professionals, this can be a real edge.

In the competitive world of financial planning, it's **a New Era in Retirement Planning.** This book serves as your roadmap and blueprint for future-proofing your business.

A New Era Opportunity: Retirement Leadership

This is more than a guide—it's a *playbook* for financial advisors ready to step up, stand out, and lead the next era of retirement planning. Inside, you'll find actionable strategies to:

- **Strengthen multigenerational relationships:** ensuring your role as a lifelong advisor across changing needs, life stages, and family transitions.
- **Bridge the longevity gap:** by fostering multigenerational learning and open dialogue, through shared knowledge, guided conversations, and advisor-led educational Longevity Literacy Gatherings.
- **Demonstrate irreplaceable value:** becoming the central point of coordination by consulting trusted professionals and building in-house expertise within your practice.

- **Leverage partnerships and AI technology:** to deepen client engagement and future-proof your practice. Become the filter and translator, helping clients navigate the noise and apply technology in ways that serve their goals. Done right, this approach builds confidence, improves transparency, and sets your practice apart in a tech-driven world.

The question is: Are you ready to lead? Are you James or are you Nicole? Read on!

PART I

The New Retirement Formula—Lifespan, Healthspan, Wealthspan

CHAPTER 1

The Blind Spot

The reports, brochures, and studies sat at the edge of James's desk, untouched, their bold titles glaring up at him like accusations: *Healthcare Costs. Longevity Trends. AI: The Disruptor. Extended and Long-Term Care Cost Projections.* Outside the window, the city skyline stretched into a crisp, blue horizon, steady and unchanging—a comforting contrast to the stack of papers threatening to upend his routine.

James leaned back in his chair, his gaze settling on the familiar skyline. The view had always offered him a sense of order—proof that some things remained constant, unmoved by the shifting tides of financial trends and client concerns. It was this sense of stability that had defined his career. Focus. Discipline. Block out the noise.

James had spent years running his practice like a racehorse guided by blinders—not because he couldn't see the obstacles ahead, but because he had trained himself to ignore anything outside his well-worn path. He felt that this singular focus —building portfolios, mitigating risk, and securing retirements —was at the core of his success. He hadn't wanted to be distracted by the landscape shifting around him, the track curving in unexpected directions. And now, forcibly for the first time, his partner, Nicole, was urging him to look past the blinders, to take in the full scope of the race before him. "I've been doing this for over twenty years," he said, leaning back, his voice steadier than he felt. "The basics haven't changed. People want to retire comfortably. They need sound investment advice to make that happen. This focus on healthcare and extended care expenses, longevity, and next-generation concerns—it's just noise."

Across the desk, Nicole sat, arms crossed, her expression sharp enough to slice through his reasoning. "It's not noise, James. It's the reality we, you, keep dodging." She leaned forward, her voice gaining an edge. "Our clients aren't just worried about their portfolios anymore. They're scared—frightened of outliving their money, of healthcare bills swallowing their savings. You think that doesn't matter?"

James glanced at the stack of materials, but his hand didn't move to pick them up. Instead, he focused his attention on Nicole, clinging to the argument that had always served him: "They come to us for results. We deliver security. All these additional concerns—they're distractions from what really matters."

Nicole's jaw tightened, and James felt the weight of her disappointment—a burden he knew he couldn't ignore. She had been his steadfast partner through market downturns and client crises, her instincts sharper than most. But now, something in her had shifted—a quiet distance settling between them that he couldn't quite name but feared all the same.

"You don't get it, do you?" Nicole said, her tone low but firm. "They value stability, yes. But stability isn't just about growing their portfolios anymore. It's about knowing they'll have enough when or for whom it matters most."

James exhaled sharply. "This feels like too much," he admitted, his voice low. "We're financial advisors, not healthcare consultants. We can't predict medical costs or control how long someone will live."

Nicole straightened, her voice calm but resolute. "We don't need to predict the future. But we do need to *prepare* for it. If we don't, someone else will. And when that happens, we won't just lose clients—we'll lose relevance."

James turned his gaze toward the window. The skyline still stood tall, unwavering. But now, it didn't feel reassuring. It felt distant.

For years, he had charged forward, trusting that his expertise and experience were enough to carry him across the finish line. But now, for the first time, he wondered: *Had he been so focused on his steady footing that he'd failed to see the track had changed?*

Her words hit harder than he expected, forcing James to look away from the window and meet her gaze. For a moment, he saw not just frustration but something deeper—a concern for their clients he couldn't dismiss. What if Nicole was right? What if the path he had always trusted wasn't enough anymore? The thought unsettled him, threatening to unravel the confidence he'd built his life on.

"I need time to think about this," he said finally, the words thick in his throat.

"Take your time," Nicole said, her voice calm but firm. She rose, a deliberate motion that signaled resolve, not retreat. Pausing just long enough to let the reality of her words settle, she added, "Just don't take too long. The world won't wait, James—it's moving on, with or without us."

CHAPTER 2

The Numbers Guy: James

James gripped the steering wheel with one hand, the other resting near the console as the familiar rhythm of his drive home unfolded. The late-afternoon light spilled across the dashboard, but his thoughts were miles away. Nicole's voice echoed in his mind from their meeting earlier that day—talk of expanding and rebranding, AI tools, digital engagement, "meeting the next generation where they are." She'd made some good points. Strong ones, actually.

Still, it rattled him.

At home, his wife was prepping dinner, and his younger son would soon be trudging in from soccer practice. His older sister was already knee-deep in midterms at college. James often thought—quietly, hopefully—that maybe one of them would one day join him in the business. The idea gave him a sense of direction, a second chapter to his life. But Nicole's push to modernize stirred a question he hadn't let himself voice out loud: *Will there even be a business worth handing over?*

He wasn't against change. He'd embraced plenty over the years. But now, driving home with the sun dropping low, what bothered him was that Nicole, his forward-thinking business partner, kept pushing to modernize the firm's focus and tools—more digital outreach, AI-enhanced planning, and new messaging that spoke to younger generations. It's not that he disagrees. On the contrary, he has always admired her drive. But, this last conversation left him wondering if they don't evolve fast enough, will there even be a practice worth handing down? It wasn't the technology—it was whether his trusted, steady way of doing things still had a place in a world where everything was speeding up.

◆◆◆

After dinner that evening, James sat alone in his study, his wife out running an errand with their son. The house seemed wrapped in a silence that only deepened his unease. Most of the reports, brochures, and studies remained untouched on his desk at the office, but one had slipped into his briefcase, almost as if it had followed him home. Now, there it sat, a silent reminder of topics he had long avoided. He had always prided himself on being practical and logical. But tonight, his thoughts wandered, untethered from the certainty that had always anchored him.

Healthcare costs. Short, Extended, and Long-term Care. Burdened Families. Staffing Storages, Clients outliving their money. Confusion about Medicare Coverages and Social Security elections. Those had always been distant problems for other firms, other advisors. But now, they felt closer. More pressing.

He absentmindedly flipped through the report, not really seeing the words. His mind wandered, drifting through memories of past clients and meetings. He thought of the concerns he'd brushed aside; the questions he had reassured them were nothing to worry about. However, those concerns now loomed larger.

He leaned back, staring at the ceiling. Nicole had mentioned Jonathan Schooler, a psychologist who studied mind-wandering and how it often led to unexpected insights. James had dismissed the idea at the time—impractical, too abstract. But now, in the quiet of his study, the clarity he had resisted for so long began to emerge as he let his mind wander.

His resistance wasn't just about the collection of reports, studies, and articles. It wasn't just about data. It was about the future. He'd avoided issues, no, he had ignored them- not because they were irrelevant, but because they were *too* relevant. They forced him to confront what he didn't want to face. Perhaps, his way of doing things—the way that had carried him through two decades of success—might not be enough anymore. Nicole was right. The world was shifting, and if they didn't shift with it, they'd be left behind, and there would be nothing of significance from all his years of work —time away from his family —to pass on to his children.

This time, when he reached for the report he had brought home, he flipped through its pages with new eyes. For the first time, he wasn't skimming. He was *seeing*. And what he saw was a future they couldn't afford to ignore.

James sat forward abruptly, the realization sparking a shift in his posture, but his mind caught on a single, heavy question: *How?* Nicole wasn't asking him to abandon the core of what they did—she was asking him to protect it, to ensure that the practice they had built could withstand the future. This wasn't about rejecting their model; it was about evolving it. Yet, the path to get there felt uncertain, tangled in complexities he wasn't sure how to unravel.

CHAPTER 3

The Visionary Partner: Nicole

That same evening, Nicole stood at the edge of the free-standing island in her kitchen, stirring a cup of chamomile tea and softly humming a tune that had been stuck in her head all day. A comforting warmth filled the house—soft light from the dimmed pendant lamps spilled over the island, and faint music from the living room created a cozy backdrop. But beneath Nicole's pensive demeanor, her mind raced with thoughts of the day.

She replayed the conversation with James over and over, each detail sharper than it needed to be. His reluctance to move forward, to evolve, felt heavier than usual. And it stung—more than she wanted to admit. It wasn't just about updating software or refreshing the website. For Nicole, modernizing the firm wasn't an option—it was a matter of survival. And maybe, if she was honest, it was also her way of staying in control.

Control had always mattered to her. Relationships, careers, friendships—she kept the upper hand wherever she could. She'd had her share of serious partners and fleeting flings, but commitment always came with strings she wasn't willing to let someone else touch, let alone pull. Still, when James dismissed her ideas with his familiar, measured tone, something inside her tightened. It was subtle, but she felt it—that quiet wave of doubt, of being sidelined. A feeling she would do almost anything to avoid. When that sensation crept in, she became sharper, quieter yet more persuasive. She'd pivot the conversation, dominate the data, flood the space with facts and underlying momentum before anyone could question her position. It wasn't a reaction—it was a reflex.

And she'd trained herself to believe it was strategy, not survival.

But the truth? That feeling didn't just sting—it haunted. It brought back the years she'd spent proving she belonged in rooms where her presence was once seen as a novelty, not a necessity. Back then, being overlooked wasn't just irritating—it was defining. And even now, after all her success, the ghost of that past had shape and voice. It left her with a kind of Imposter Syndrome she thought she had buried long ago.

Whether she acknowledged it or not, that fear—the fear of being unseen—ran the show. It didn't just influence her decisions; it formed the spine of her ambition. It was the silent force behind every late night, every bold pitch, every drive to modernize the firm before someone else told her what she could or couldn't do. She wasn't that 'newbie' anymore. She'd earned her seat at the table. But that old voice hadn't left. It just whispered now, softer but still there.

Whether she admitted it or not, that fear—the fear of being unseen—shaped everything. It didn't just show up at work; it trailed her home, forming the basis of personal and lifestyle decisions, and it leaked into every relationship that started strong but ended with her pulling away. The idea of giving up even an ounce of autonomy was not in her DNA. She'd joked about it, even worn it like a badge—*I like my space, I like my freedom.* But deep down, it was more than preference. It was protection. *Don't let them decide for you. Don't let them take the lead.*

And even now, standing alone in her kitchen, that silent voice was anything but quiet—it dominated her thoughts, shouting beneath the calm, steady rhythm of her everyday life. It was ironic, really. She had built her reputation on empathy, on her uncanny ability to sense when a client was overwhelmed, uncertain, or holding something back. She made them feel safe, in control, and grounded.

What they didn't know—what she barely admitted to herself—was that same desire for control lived inside her too. She didn't just understand it. She *embodied* it. Her ability to read clients so well came, in part, from her own experience of living in that emotional space. Wanting clarity. Wanting certainty. Wanting a say in how things turned out.

In the end, it wasn't a contradiction. It was her edge. The need that drove her was the same one that built trust with every client she met. They could feel it. She wasn't just leading them—she was walking the same tightrope.

But tonight, even the tea's calming aroma couldn't fully settle her thoughts. Nicole leaned against the island's counter, her reflection in the darkened window catching her attention. A sassy quip about her need for beauty sleep flitted to her lips, but she didn't say it aloud. She was too consumed by the quiet gravity of what had been building inside her for months.

Retirement planning, or admittedly, financial planning in general, wasn't what it used to be. It wasn't just about tax-efficient strategies or optimizing withdrawals. It was about life—messy, unpredictable, beautiful life. And as the clients they served faced longer lifespans and more complex family dynamics, the firm's approach needed to evolve.

She thought back to the meeting with James that she had earlier that day. Predictably, he had pushed back—driven by his unwavering commitment to logic and precision. It wasn't resistance for its own sake; it was James safeguarding the integrity of their work, the foundation they had built together. Nicole understood that, even if their approaches differed, their goals were the same. Nicole felt more encouraged this time since she had seen the flicker of understanding in his eyes, the glimmer of curiosity that hinted at something deeper. It was a start, she thought. With James, it was always about planting the seed.

Her phone buzzed on the counter, interrupting her reverie. A client had emailed, thanking her for the talk they'd had about caregiving costs for aging parents. Nicole smiled faintly, but it was a bittersweet expression. The gratitude in the email reminded her of how much more there was to do—how many families still faced those uncharted waters alone, without the tools to navigate them.

She sighed, her tea forgotten as she reached for her iPad. Nicole's mind worked best when her pen was in motion. Sketching ideas, jotting questions, linking concepts—it was how she had always brought clarity to the nebulous. Tonight, she scribbled furiously, the words spilling from her pen faster than she could fully capture them.

"Connection," she wrote at the top of the page. Underneath, she began listing ways to strengthen it not just between clients and their finances, but between clients and their lives, between families and their futures. It wasn't enough to plan for retirement; they had to plan for resilience, for joy, for the unexpected.

James might have been the firm's compass, ensuring they stayed on course. But Nicole was the wind beneath their sails, propelling them toward horizons they hadn't dared to imagine. Together, they made the perfect team: his practicality grounded her vision, her energy ignited his precision.

As the evening wore on, Nicole's iPad filled with ideas. By the time she closed it, her tea had gone cold, but her resolve was warm and steady. Tomorrow, she'd sit down with James again. Nicole's push for a more holistic approach was no longer just a suggestion. It was a mission.

As she turned off the lights, her reflection in the window disappeared, leaving only the quiet night behind. But in her mind, the vision burned bright—a future where the firm didn't just manage wealth or fund retirements but helped to shape lifestyles. A future where she, James, and their team didn't just plan—they transformed. They would move from transaction to transformation.

CHAPTER 4

The Wake-Up Call

The Illusion of a Steady Plan

The office was unusually quiet as James waited for Mr. Whitmore. A loyal client for decades, Mr. Whitmore had always been a steady presence, his trust unwavering. But today, something felt off—he couldn't quite name it, but felt it low in his stomach, like a shift in pressure before a storm. When Mr. Whitmore entered the room, James couldn't help but note that the familiar sight of Whitmore's confident stride had softened with age. He moved more deliberately now, and though his eyes still held the sharpness James admired, there was an undercurrent of apprehension. But it wasn't Mr. Whitmore's entrance that sent James's pulse racing. It was the abrupt arrival of his children, Bryan and Sarah. Their presence didn't just dominate the room; it transformed it, shifting the air to something sharper, taut with unspoken stakes.

Bryan, every inch the executor of his father's ambitions, strode in with the precision of someone piecing together a fragile puzzle. Each movement was deliberate, his gaze steady yet probing, cutting through the room's silence with the focus of someone stepping into a role he hadn't asked for as he settled into a chair with quiet resolve.

Sarah followed, a study in composed elegance. Her tailored exterior betrayed nothing, yet her polite smile hovered like a veil over something unsteady—a storm just restrained. It wasn't the warmth of her expression that James noticed, but the way her eyes scanned the room, missing nothing.

Their presence wasn't just unexpected; it unsettled something in James, a tension he couldn't yet name. A line drawn in the sand that James hadn't seen coming—and couldn't yet fathom how to cross.

"Good to see you, Mr. Whitmore. And welcome—nice to have the whole family here today," James said, masking his growing unease with practiced warmth. "I assume you received the last statement showing the portfolio is in good shape?"

Mr. Whitmore nodded, but his usual warmth seemed muted. "The portfolio's fine, James, but my kids have some concerns. We've been talking about the future—whether there are risks we've overlooked."

Bryan clasped his hands tightly, his knuckles slightly whitening as he spoke. "We know Dad's in relatively good health now, but we're worried the current plan doesn't account for the rising cost of healthcare, especially extended care. Have you run any scenarios for long-term care or a prolonged illness? Because if something happens to Dad or Mom, it *obviously* could drain the portfolio faster than expected."

James felt a surge of defensiveness at the word 'obviously' but maintained his composure. "We've always focused on protecting your father's assets and ensuring his retirement and legacy are secure. We've discussed long-term care before and built in some contingencies."

Sarah's gaze didn't waver. She tucked a loose strand of hair behind her ear, the motion quick and precise, as though grounding herself before speaking. "But are those contingencies enough? If Dad needs to withdraw more than expected for home modifications or care, are there tax implications?

It's not just about today's comfort—it's about ensuring they don't outlive their money, especially if major or prolonged health events arise."

The shift in the conversation was palpable. What had begun as a standard review was now unraveling into a discussion James hadn't fully anticipated. The foundation of his confident strategies was beginning to crack under the weight of questions he'd long avoided.

Mr. Whitmore finally spoke, his voice tinged with weariness. "I just want to make sure I'm leaving something behind for them and my grandchildren. That's what matters most to me. We've worked on this plan together, James, and I need to know if there are risks that we haven't fully addressed that could jeopardize that legacy."

This concern, which ties wealthcare and healthcare to longevity, was one James had started to hear in various forms lately, but today it hit differently. It echoed the very concerns Nicole had voiced just days earlier, only now, they weren't theoretical. They were sitting across from him, eyes full of anxiety and trepidation, turning her warning into something undeniably real. James nodded, feeling the full weight of the family's collective gaze on him. A heavy silence settled over the room. The children weren't just questioning his methods—they were questioning whether the financial plan he had built for their parents could withstand the inevitable risks that come with longevity.

The conversation had exposed a complex web of challenges—rising healthcare costs, extended care, the rapid depletion of resources from unexpected events, and looming tax implications that could erode Mr. Whitmore's carefully built retirement plan.

James sensed that Whitmore's children worried about the emotional and financial toll that far-reaching changes inherent in caregiving could exact, but for Mr. Whitmore, the burden ran deeper. Quietly, he wrestled with a fear he dared not voice: the prospect of outliving the wealth meant to secure his wife's care, to support his children, and, most poignantly, to safeguard a future for his grandchildren. To fail in this, he feared, would mean forfeiting not just his wealth, but the legacy he had spent a lifetime building.

James stood, smoothing the edge of his notepad, and met each of their eyes with a steadiness he hadn't quite felt until now.

"I hear all of you," he said, his voice calm but resolute. *"You're asking the right questions—and I promise you, we're going to take another look. A deeper look."*

It wasn't just a promise to the Whitmores. It was a turning point—for his practice, for his partnership with Nicole, and for the legacy he hoped to protect.

◆◆◆

As the meeting wrapped up, tension hung in the air. Their concerns were valid, and James could no longer ignore the implications. Before leaving, Mr. Whitmore asked for a private word with James, leaving Bryan and Sarah lingering in the conference room. Sarah scrolled through her phone, her polished demeanor intact, while Bryan ran a hand through his hair—an unconscious tell she'd long recognized as his version of unraveling. The tension in the room was palpable, thick, and unwelcoming.

Bryan broke the silence, his voice low but weighted with concern. *"I know Dad says he's in good shape financially, but have you noticed he's... just not moving through things the way he used to?"*

Sarah caught the subtext immediately, and the validation rattled her. She had sensed it too—that quieter pace, the way her dad seemed to take longer before answering, choosing his words with extra care. It wasn't just age. It was something else. She couldn't or didn't want to give it a name. So, she attributed it to something unspoken, like just his being worried about something he hadn't shared.

"I know Dad says he's in good shape financially," Bryan went on, " but have you thought about how much caregiving could cost us? And I don't just mean money."

Sarah looked up, her eyes narrowing in a question. "You mean beyond what Dad or Mom can afford?"

"Exactly." Bryan leaned in, resting his elbows on his knees. "I've been reading this book—*How Not to Pull Your Family Apart: A Practical Guide to Caregiving and Financial Stability.* The author identifies family caregivers as the 'Shadow Caregiving System,' -the unpaid, behind-the-scenes stuff families do without even realizing they've taken on the role of caregiver. "Things like constantly checking in on Dad—just to make sure everything's okay. Offering to accompany him to doctor's appointments, not just to be polite, but to actually be there as a second pair of ears or to take notes... even though doctors send summaries now, I still want to go. Not for the notes, but to make sure we both understand what just happened in the room. Then there's coordinating his appointments, tracking down prescriptions, Googling every new medication, sitting on hold with insurance companies for hours... It's already happening. And no one's calling it what it is. It's creeping in, and we haven't acknowledged it-and apparently neither has Dad or his advisor."

Sarah's expression shifted—less defensive now, more thoughtful. She looked at her brother as if seeing him a little differently.

"I didn't realize you were carrying that much," she said, her voice quieter, almost unsure. "I thought you were just helping out where you could."

Bryan exhaled hard, not in anger but in release. "That's the thing. I didn't realize it either, not at first. It's not some big, dramatic shift. It just builds. One small task turns into a dozen. Then suddenly, in the middle of a work presentation, all I can think about is whether Dad remembered his medication."

He paused, then added, "Caregiving isn't just about cutting checks or showing up on holidays. It's being 'on' all the time—mentally, emotionally, everywhere. At work, at home, for our own families, and now, for them."

The reality settled over them both, heavy and unspoken. Sarah bit her lip. "We need to get ahead of this, Bryan. If James can't adapt, we need to find someone who understands how all of this affects retirement and legacy plans. Mom and Dad worked too hard for us to ignore this."

Bryan nodded. "James is good at what he does, but he's stuck in an old mindset—focused on budgeting and investments. He isn't considering the unpredictable impact of aging on his financial plans. When a health crisis hits, slowly or suddenly, everything changes—money, relationships, time, energy."

Sarah leaned back, her gaze steady but reflective. "We need to start this conversation now, before it's too late. It's not just about protecting their money—it's about protecting their peace of mind."

Bryan's tone softened; his voice tinged with concern. "You're right. We owe it to them to make sure they have a say in their future. We need to sit down with them, hear what they want, and how they envision their care, and then ensure their planner is planning for it. They deserve that."

As their father and James re-entered the room, the siblings fell silent. James made his polite goodbyes, but the tension clung to him as he returned to his desk. For the first time, he truly questioned whether sticking to his 'traditional' methods was a risk he could afford to take. The concerns from Whitmore's children had rattled him; their honesty had left a mark he couldn't ignore.

As James sat alone in his office after the Whitmores left, their concerns replayed in his mind like an unwelcome echo. He didn't doubt the validity of their worries. Could it be that his steadfast strategies—strategies that had built the firm's success—were no longer enough? This wasn't just about managing portfolios anymore—it was about confronting the stark, unpredictable realities that aging could impose: the potential and substantial costs of healthcare, the creeping inevitability of long-term care, and the hidden emotional toll of shifting family dynamics. A sudden illness or the need for around-the-clock care could dismantle even the most meticulously planned finances and legacy, while unanticipated living arrangements—such as downsizing, retrofitting a home, or moving into assisted living—add layers of investment and tax complexity. These weren't just logistical challenges; they were seismic shifts that carried the power to unravel not only financial security but the sense of dignity and peace every family strived to protect.

Yet, James found himself resisting the cracks forming, the nagging sense that his once-reliable playbook might not be enough. The very thought of overhauling his approach felt like an admission of failure—something James had spent his entire career avoiding. He'd built his reputation on steadiness, on being the unflinching hand at the wheel during shifting, unpredictable markets, or when clients panicked. If he acknowledged the Whitmores' concerns too deeply, it would mean stepping into uncharted territory—territory he wasn't sure he was equipped to navigate. That was the real rub. It was easier, safer, to chalk up their anxiety to generational impatience, to dismiss their questions as overthinking rather than confronting the uneasy truth they represented.

CHAPTER 5

The Tipping Point

The Clash of Two Perspectives

The next morning, James arrived at the office early. He paused briefly, glancing toward Nicole's door, as he headed for the sanctuary of his own office. Everything was just as he liked it—precise, controlled, organized. His desk was clear, his chair angled perfectly, the framed photos of his family lined up with quiet symmetry. But the order of the room didn't settle him the way it usually did. He sat down and inhaled deeply. The conversation he'd been avoiding could wait no longer. He opened his laptop and pinged her: *"Would you mind stopping by when it's convenient?"*

After leaving James's office, Nicole dropped into her chair with an exasperated thud. The city skyline stretched before her, gleaming and inspiring, but its usual spark failed to register. Instead, her mind replayed James's almost dismissive remarks about Mr. Whitmore's "self-absorbed" children, each word stoking the simmering frustration she fought to contain.

Challenges fueled Nicole. Her sharp wit, coupled with a vast social network, made her the firm's rainmaker. Clients sought her out because she had an uncanny ability to read people, often identifying their needs before they voiced them. Nicole exuded a magnetic energy that kept her phone constantly buzzing with invitations, inquiries, and referrals.

Yet beneath her lively exterior was a mind as sharp as her instincts. Nicole wasn't just the firm's public face—she was its engine for growth. And right now, growth felt like a battle she was waging alone. James was brilliant. His precision in managing portfolios had kept the firm thriving for years. But Nicole saw what he refused to: clients wanted more than just solid investment or retirement advice. They needed guidance on aging parents, career transitions, tax strategies, and navigating the complexities of retirement. Yet, every time she broached the idea of expanding the team or bringing in specialists, James would brush her off with his familiar refrain: "Why fix what isn't broken?"

She thought back to their recent conversation about hiring a younger advisor to connect with the next generation of clients. James hadn't even looked up from his meticulously arranged desk. "We've built this brand on trust and expertise. Bringing in someone new could dilute that," he had said.

Nicole had swallowed her frustration then, but now, back in her own office, the memory stoked her impatience. "The cracks are already showing," she muttered to herself. "If we don't adapt, the whole thing could collapse."

She knew James's resistance wasn't just about logistics—it was about order. The idea of relinquishing even a sliver of the familiar, established business made him uneasy. But Nicole also understood James deeply. He valued legacy and loyalty, and she knew if she framed her vision in terms of preserving those values, she might finally break through his defenses.

Nicole stood, smoothing the front of her blazer, resolve hardening her features. The day's next meeting loomed, and she wasn't about to let it go to waste. She would keep pushing—gently but firmly. James might be the rock that kept the firm grounded, but she was the force propelling it forward. In her mind, the future was bright—if only she could get him to take the first step toward it.

◆◆◆

Nicole's Vision

The two partners had always been a balance of opposites, a yin and yang that had kept the firm strong. Nicole was the embodiment of charisma and social networking, while James represented precision and efficiency. Tall and composed, with a sharp gaze and neatly trimmed hair, he was the picture of an analytical mind, someone who thrived on optimizing financial outcomes. His office reflected his meticulous nature—files were perfectly organized, and every pen was in its designated place.

But as Nicole passed his office on her way out, her eyes fell on the stack of studies, reports, and brochures she'd left on his desk weeks ago, now partially hidden beneath a neat pile of client files. She paused, staring for a moment before continuing down the hall on her way out of the office, her resolve hardening.

"We've come too far to let this firm stagnate because we're stuck in yesterday," she thought. "And I'm not about to let that happen—not even if it means dragging James, kicking and screaming, into the future."

Later that night, as Nicole unloaded the dishwasher, a quiet smile tugged at her lips. She couldn't help but notice the abundance of wine glasses, each one a small testament to the lively, laughter-filled evening. The rhythmic clinking as she placed them back on the shelf had an oddly soothing quality, offering her mind the space to wander. James's words from earlier resurfaced, playing over and over in her mind like the background hum of a melody she couldn't shake. Her brow furrowed slightly. Could she ever convince him to see the bigger picture?

And then, it happened.

The idea hit her so suddenly it felt almost theatrical, like the perfect punchline delivered in a moment of stillness. Nicole froze, a wine glass suspended midair, her breath catching as a thread of clarity unraveled and stretched across her thoughts. Slowly, deliberately, she lowered the glass onto the counter, her pulse quickening as she began to grasp the significance of what had just clicked.

Clients didn't want only financial security, as important as that is—they wanted a plan that understood them holistically. Aging. Health. Wealth. Family. Longevity. Given the constant barrage of information—articles, updates, videos, commercials, market alerts—clients were more overwhelmed than ever. They didn't need more data. They needed someone to distill it, to personalize it, to make it make sense in the context of their own lives. Someone who could see the whole picture and say, *"Here's what matters for you."* Because beneath the surface, it was all connected—finances, health, family, fears about the future—in ways they hadn't dared to articulate but desperately needed someone to understand and bring into focus. Nicole's mind churned, the pieces snapping into place like a perfectly completed puzzle. This was still about managing risks and balancing portfolios, but it needed to connect to lifespans, healthspans, and wealthspans in relatable, client-friendly doses.

Her heart raced as the implications crystallized. This insight would change everything. It reminded her of something she'd heard on an old 30 Rock episode, about the "Shower Technique," where your sharpest ideas ambushed you during moments of distraction. Well, tonight it wasn't a shower—it was the mundane task of dishwasher duty. But the impact was no less profound.

In that instant, Nicole saw her path forward. The next meeting with James wasn't just another chance to argue her case; it was the moment to refine the firm's future. What clients needed most wasn't just answers—it was help uncovering the right questions. Often, they didn't know what they didn't know. They weren't just looking for facts; they needed someone to connect the dots, to gently surface the blind spots and concerns they hadn't thought to voice. The real value came in those moments of clarity—when an advisor helped them understand not only the plan, but the deeper "why" behind it. She exhaled slowly. There was no turning back now. And just like that, Nicole had found her voice—and the blueprint for the future.

◆◆◆

James's Stubborn Reluctance

Later that afternoon, long after his meeting with Nicole had ended and the buzz of the office had quieted, James sat alone at his desk, the Whitmore file still open in front of him. The numbers stared back at him—solid, well-structured, consistent. But after everything Nicole had pressed him to consider, and after what Mr. Whitmore had confided in him, they no longer felt like enough.

He leaned back, letting his mind settle into the memory of that private moment—the moment he had left Whitmore's children in the conference room and had sequestered Whitmore and himself in his office. Whitmore hadn't said much at first. Just a small, hesitant smile and a look James hadn't seen in him before: fear.

"James," he'd begun, his voice steady but quieter than usual, "I didn't want to bring this up with the kids in the room… but I need to tell you something."

He'd paused, fingers brushing the edge of his chair, then continued, slower now, like each word was being weighed before spoken.

"It's not just the slowing down—I can live with that. I move more carefully now, more deliberately. But my mind… James, I'm forgetting things. Names I can't recall, appointments I almost miss. And it's not just names or dates. Sometimes I walk into a room and don't know how I got there or how to get out of there. Sometimes I look at my wife and think, *'What if she has to handle everything if I start losing …?'*" His voice trailed off without finishing.

James found himself filling in the sentence, surprised by the profound sadness that swept over him.

The raw honesty of the moment had stopped James cold. Mr. Whitmore had always been the picture of control—dignified, sharp, prepared. Now, he sounded like a man bracing for a future he could feel coming before anyone else could see it.

"I've read the stats," he said. "I've seen the costs. Memory care, long-term support—it can strip away everything you've saved. And I can't stop thinking about that big house we've loved for so long. If she's alone in it… if she gets sick too…"

His voice caught slightly, but he pressed on.

"This isn't just about me or even my wife, although that is a major concern. It's also about what comes after, Bryan, Sarah, and the grandkids. I've spent a lifetime building something meant to protect them. But if I let this slip by—if we don't plan for it—*I could be handing them a mess, not a legacy.*"

Now, in the quiet space of his office, James felt the full weight of that conversation settle in. This wasn't about market fluctuations or risk tolerance. It was about love. About dignity. About fear of becoming a burden when all you've ever planned for is to protect. This was about the hard, unspoken truths that every carefully built plan eventually runs into.

And it was up to him to respond—not just with charts, but with care. With clarity. With a plan that truly accounted for what mattered most to his client, a loyal client whom he cared about.

He leaned back in his chair, his mind searching to grasp what was happening in real time.

James tapped the pen against the edge of the file and exhaled slowly. Mr. Whitmore wasn't asking for a miracle. He was asking for a guide—someone to see what he saw coming and help carry the weight before it fell on the people he loved most.

It was a reasonable request—a human one. And yet, it left James feeling unsteady.

This was more than he was used to holding. The numbers were still solid. The investments sound good. He told himself that it should be enough. That's the part he knew how to manage—where formulas held and logic prevailed. But this? This was different. It was murky, emotional, and undefined. And that made him want to retreat to the certainty of spreadsheets and projections, to reassert the order he knew.

Even as he tried to compartmentalize it, the weight of what Mr. Whitmore had shared pressed in around the edges. He could file the paperwork, but not the responsibility. He tried to box it up, label it *outside the scope.* But Mr. Whitmore's words had found a crack. The unease he felt wasn't just noise anymore—it was something deeper, something he didn't yet know how to solve. And that unsettled him far more than he was willing to admit.

The Spark Behind the Smile

James was determined not to get caught up in one client's problem and turn it into a reason to change the order of things. Nicole swept into the room, radiating purpose and the unmistakable energy of someone who had already conquered her to-do list earlier in the day. In her case, probably before 10 a.m. Her smile was bright, eyes sparkling with that glint of mischief that usually preceded one of her signature sharp-witted remarks.

"Morning, partner!" she chimed, leaning casually against the doorframe, arms crossed. "I've been thinking… and don't worry, I've already braced myself for your stubborn resistance."

James sighed, glancing up with mild exasperation. He recognized that tone all too well. It was the one Nicole used right before launching into another one of her "big ideas." This was becoming a pattern. He straightened the papers on his desk—a subconscious reflex—hoping that the sense of order might ground him in the familiar. "Nicole, if this is about Whitmore and his kids, we've already discussed—"

"OK, keep your shirt on," Nicole interrupted with a grin. "I'm not here to turn the office into some Jetsons' retirement planning mecca overnight. But let's face it—clients are expecting more these days. It's not just about the portfolio anymore. It's about the bigger picture. And lucky for you, I'm ready to do the heavy lifting." She waved a folder as if it were some golden ticket. "I've got a couple of ideas for how we can modernize things. Don't worry, I'll handle the research. Think of it as adding a little sparkle to what we already do so well."

James leaned back in his chair, his arms crossing in quiet defiance. His gaze flicked to his desk, every pen, folder, and paper meticulously arranged—a fortress of order in a world that seemed to demand chaos. This was his anchor, his proof that precision and discipline could outlast any storm. Nicole's suggestions, however well-meaning, felt like an assault on that stability.

"Nicole, our clients don't care about 'sparkle.' They care about returns. We've built this firm on solid, no-nonsense retirement planning grounded in investment management. These extras are just distractions."

Nicole's smile didn't falter, but her eyes narrowed with playful intensity. "Sure, but what if those 'extras' are why Whitmore's kids are ready to jump ship, despite the solid portfolio? They want to know their dad's plan accounts for more than just investments, where wealth and health intersect. If we don't offer those answers, someone else will."

Frustration flickered in James's eyes as his hands slightly gripped the edge of the desk. He rarely allowed himself to get flustered in conversations like this. Normally, he met Nicole's enthusiasm with calm pragmatism, deflecting her ideas with reason. Whitmore's words—quiet, personal, laced with fear—were still echoing in the back of his mind. He had been trying to bury them under reports and routines, but they lingered, sharper than he expected. And now, Nicole's timing and certainty grated against a part of him still too unsettled to name. He was on edge. "We're not some boutique firm tossing out trendy buzzwords to make clients feel better. We focus on what we're good at—solid, grounded retirement planning. You handle the client relations, and I'll ensure their money is managed wisely," James said, his tone more clipped than he intended.

Nicole didn't miss a beat. Her smile didn't falter, and she didn't push back. But she caught it—something in his voice, a tension that didn't match the conversation. She noted it, tucked it away, and carried on. That was her strength—reading the room without letting the room read her.

"And that's exactly why I'm suggesting we enhance what we do—so they keep coming back. I'm not talking about abandoning our strengths. I'm talking about evolving them. We don't need to reinvent the wheel, James, but we could at least give it a little power steering."

James couldn't help but chuckle at her analogy, but the amusement didn't last. His gaze drifted back to his desk, where every folder, every sheet of paper was perfectly aligned. It was how he liked things—orderly, predictable, efficient. But was that what his clients wanted?

Before the thought could take root, he shook it off. "Look, Nicole, I appreciate the enthusiasm, but we're not reinventing anything. We're sticking to what's worked for years. I don't need a bunch of bells and whistles distracting me—or our clients."

Nicole stepped farther into the room, her expression a careful balance of calm and urgency. "James," she began, her voice low but steady, "this isn't about tearing down what we've built. It's about ensuring it has a future."

She paused, her gaze intent. "Trust and credibility—those are the cornerstones of what we do. But trust isn't static. It evolves. Clients don't just want to know we're managing their money; they want to feel we're looking out for the bigger picture. They're looking for someone who sees beyond the numbers—who's willing to ask the right questions, so if there's something important going on with their health or family, they have the space to share it. It's about creating the kind of relationship where they feel understood, not just advised." Her voice softened, yet it carried a weight that couldn't be ignored. "It's about showing them we're not just keeping up; we're anticipating their needs before they even articulate them. That's what will keep us relevant. That's what will keep them loyal." Nicole stepped closer, her tone sharpening. "If we stay where we are, James, we'll lose the very credibility that got us here. But if we evolve—if we show them that we're ahead of the curve, thinking holistically, creating solutions, offering solutions that others aren't offering—that's how we win their trust in a way no one else can."

She straightened, her resolve clear in every word. "This isn't just about staying competitive. It's about becoming indispensable. AI can throw out numbers, run projections, even build scenarios faster than we ever could—but it can't ask the right questions. It can't sense when a client is holding something back or help them untangle what really matters to them. That's where we make the difference. That's what makes us irreplaceable."

James shifted in his seat, the tension knotting his shoulders. She was right, and deep down, he knew it. But admitting that felt like surrendering a part of himself—a part of what had defined his career, but he simply wasn't ready.

"You're a smart guy, James," Nicole continued, her voice carrying the warmth of camaraderie and the edge of challenge. "But right now, you're an anchor—not grounding us, but holding us back. The tide's shifting, and if we don't move with it, we'll be left behind. I'm offering to do the work. All I'm asking is that we stay open to the possibility that there's more we could offer. You know, just in case the world doesn't stay the same forever."

With a determined flash in her eyes, Nicole turned to leave, her words hanging in the air like a challenge. "Fine. I'll do the research and come up with a couple of different approaches. But don't expect me to let this go just because you're clinging to the past like it's a life preserver."

The door clicked shut behind her, and the silence that followed was deafening. James sat motionless, the stillness of his office pressing in like a weight. The steady tick of the clock punctuated the quiet, each beat a reminder of time slipping by—time he could no longer ignore.

His gaze drifted to the studies and articles that Nicole had left weeks ago. One was just visible beneath the stack of perfectly aligned folders. Its glossy edge jutted out, slightly askew, an affront to the order he clung to like a lifeline. James reached out, his hand hovering above the pile, but stopped short. He couldn't bring himself to touch it—not yet.

The world outside his office window moved on, indifferent to his hesitation. Maybe Nicole was right. Maybe clients were beginning to care about more than just steady returns. Perhaps Whitmore and his children were not an isolated case. Maybe they wanted something James had spent his career avoiding: a plan that accounted for life's uncertainties, the messy, unpredictable truths of aging and caregiving. He exhaled slowly, the thought coiling in his chest like a knot he couldn't untangle. For now, he turned back to his work, straightening the papers on his desk with a practiced precision that felt more like a ritual than a necessity. Order. Predictability. These were the things that had defined his success. But as the silence deepened, it carried a weight he couldn't shake—a heaviness that settled over him like an unanswered question, growing louder with each passing second.

James's eyes flicked back to the materials Nicole had left for him to read. They waited, a silent demand for acknowledgment. He adjusted the stack again, aligning the edges with meticulous care, as if that small act could restore balance to the shifting ground beneath him. But the unease lingered, an uninvited guest in the sanctuary of his office.

◆◆◆

Answering the Call to Innovate

A few days had passed since their last conversation, and though the tension between James and Nicole had eased, something had undoubtedly shifted. James found himself cautiously curious—still skeptical about the need for change but unable to shake a growing interest in what Nicole had uncovered. The doubts that once felt fleeting now clung to his thoughts, gently eroding his usual certainty.

They met in the conference room, where the soft morning light filtered through large windows, casting a warm glow over the polished table. The room, filled with memories of past victories and occasional growing pains, had an air of both familiarity and quiet anticipation. Nicole was already there, a neatly arranged folder before her, steam curling upward from her coffee—a quiet signal of the early hour. The scene was routine, yet today it carried an importance James hadn't anticipated.

When James entered, Nicole greeted him with calm, focused energy. Her usual playful banter had been replaced with a more serious demeanor. "Alright, James," she began, her voice steady, "I know you have reasons to stick with what's been working. I'm not here to bulldoze that. Let's just talk it through, and then I'll show you what I found."

She paused for a moment, studying his expression before continuing. "What do you think is the biggest fear our clients face as they approach retirement?"

James leaned back in his chair, crossing his arms. "I suppose it's running out of money. But we've got that covered with our financial planning tools."

Nicole nodded thoughtfully. "True, financial planning is crucial. But is that the only thing on their minds? What happens when healthcare costs rise unexpectedly?"

James frowned. He didn't like where this was heading. "We can't control healthcare costs, Nicole. That's not our job. We focus on wealth management, not healthcare."

"I get that," Nicole replied, undeterred. "But think about it from the client's perspective. If they're worried about healthcare eating into their savings, do you think they'll feel truly secure, even if we've optimized their portfolio?"

James's discomfort was apparent, his fingers tapping the table. "Our job is to maximize their wealth. If we start worrying about every potential cost, we'll spread ourselves too thin."

Nicole leaned forward slightly, her tone patient but more insistent. "I hear you. But what if we could help them feel more prepared for those costs? Wouldn't that make them more confident about their retirement and, in turn, more satisfied with our service?"

James shifted in his seat, clearly wrestling with her point. "Maybe. But where do we draw the line? We're not healthcare advisors."

"No, we're not," Nicole agreed, "but we are advisors who care about their overall well-being. What if we built connections with specialists—people who could guide our clients through healthcare challenges? Wouldn't that strengthen their trust in us?"

James shook his head, still resistant. "I don't see how this fits into our model, Nicole. We're here to manage wealth, not health."

Nicole paused, sensing a need to shift her approach. "James, when we put up walls between what we do and the other aspects of our clients' lives, what's on the other side of those walls? What might we be missing?"

James was silent for a moment, caught off guard. His brow furrowed as he considered her words. "I guess… we might overlook how those other aspects could impact their financial stability."

"Exactly," Nicole said, sensing a crack in his resistance. "And if we miss that, we risk making decisions that don't fully protect their future. Our clients trust us to see the bigger picture, don't they?"

James rubbed his temple, visibly conflicted. "I suppose. But integrating this into our approach is a big shift. It's risky."

"Is it riskier than ignoring it and leaving our clients exposed?" Nicole countered, her tone calm yet pointed. "Wouldn't the real risk be in failing to adapt to their needs as they age?"

James exhaled deeply, grappling with the idea. "You make it sound so straightforward, but it's not. We've built this firm on a specific philosophy—shifting it could be dangerous."

"It could be," Nicole agreed. "But consider this: if our clients feel unprepared for healthcare costs, and that insecurity leads them to question our entire plan, wouldn't that be even more dangerous? What's the point of building wealth if they fear their healthcare needs will deplete it?"

James stared at her, the tension in his face softening. "I hadn't thought of it that way. You're saying we need to help them feel prepared for what comes with longevity."

"Exactly," Nicole replied, her tone encouraging. "Building longevity literacy doesn't mean we lose focus—it means we broaden our perspective to protect what matters to our clients."

James nodded slightly. "It's a lot to take in, but I see the value in this approach."

Nicole smiled warmly. "That's all I'm asking for. Let's keep exploring it together. I think this could make all the difference for our clients—and for us."

In the days that followed, their conversation lingered in James's mind, challenging his deeply ingrained perspective. Nicole's questions resurfaced, urging him to reconsider the firm's future direction. He revisited their discussion often, not just during the workday, but in quieter, reflective moments.

Weeks later, as James and Nicole sat down to continue their dialogue, the tension that had once dominated their exchanges had lessened. James's posture had shifted—there was less guardedness, more curiosity. Nicole noticed the change, the softening of his usual reserve.

Breaking the silence, Nicole spoke first, her voice confident but gentle. "I did some digging, and I think you'll like what I found."

"Go on," James replied, a hint of interest creeping into his tone.

Nicole opened the folder in front of her, the rustle of papers filling the stillness. "I investigated firms that made small but significant adjustments to their retirement planning strategies—nothing radical, just thoughtful shifts that helped them stay ahead. It's not about throwing out what we know; it's about adding layers that enhance what we already do well."

A faint smile crossed James's face as he scanned the documents. "So, how do we manage this without overwhelming the client—or ourselves?"

Nicole's grin widened. "It's simpler than you think. We're not talking about adding more work; we're talking about positioning ourselves as forward-thinking partners. We guide clients through issues like the tax implications of healthcare withdrawals, rising Medicare costs, and extended care scenarios. We integrate these elements into our core strategy without losing focus on their investment goals."

She paused, letting the gravity of her words sink in. "While we can't predict every twist in healthcare costs, we can give clients the tools to navigate those uncertainties. Even our high-net-worth clients could see their liquidity strained by unexpected long-term care costs. We need to show their families that we're thinking ahead, mitigating risks before they become crises."

James nodded, his fingers tapping the table, a habitual gesture of contemplation. He wasn't fully convinced, but Nicole's logic was sound. This wasn't the disruptive change he'd feared; it was an evolution that respected their strengths while addressing new realities.

Sensing his openness, Nicole softened her tone. "Look, I'm not asking for full commitment yet. But what if we ran a pilot? Test one or two ideas with clients who are already inclined toward this kind of planning. You take the lead. I trust your instincts."

James blinked, surprised by her offer. He had expected more pushback, but instead, Nicole was handing him control. The steady tick of the clock filled the quiet as he weighed her proposal. For the first time, adapting felt less like a threat and more like an opportunity.

He took a deep breath and reached for the folder. "Alright, let's see what this might look like. I'll identify a few clients, and we'll start there."

Nicole's smile grew wider, satisfaction more than triumph lighting her eyes. "I think you'll like where this leads. And if not, we can reconsider—no harm done."

As they wrapped up the meeting, James found himself warming to Nicole's ideas in a way he hadn't expected. It wasn't about abandoning the firm's guiding principles; it was about refining them. For the first time, integrating new strategies didn't feel like losing ground—it felt like an opportunity to grow.

They turned their attention to lunch, the smell of fresh sandwiches mingling with the rich aroma of coffee. Their conversation drifted to lighter topics, but the sense of newfound alignment was unmistakable. A quiet turning point had been reached in their partnership.

Later, back in his office, James's gaze fell on the stack of brochures still lying untouched on his desk. The morning light filtered through the blinds, casting shadows across the papers. For the first time in years, his mind buzzed with the stirrings of new possibilities—ideas he hadn't considered in a long while.

CHAPTER 6

Recalibrating North

The next morning, James stepped into the office and was struck by how quiet it felt, not in sound, but in certainty. Everything was in its place, yet nothing felt anchored.

He retreated to the familiarity of his office, but the order and routine that usually grounded him offered no relief. Papers lay untouched on his desk. Outside, the skyline shimmered in the morning light, calm and composed—but it brought no clarity.

Nicole's voice still echoed in his mind: *"You've become an anchor—not grounding us, but holding us back."*

It wasn't the sharpness of her words that had unsettled him—it was the truth behind them.

For years, James had navigated his work with a reliable moral compass: focus on growth, minimize risk, and protect the nest egg. It had always felt right. But now that compass felt misaligned, its needle twitched with uncertainty. The meeting with the Whitmores hadn't just challenged his methods—it had shaken his sense of direction. And Nicole's vision—

bold, human, future-focused—was starting to feel less like disruption and more like guidance. A map to somewhere he hadn't even known he needed to go.

And now, for the first time in years, James didn't know what should come next.

He turned to his inbox. At the top was a message from Nicole, sent late the night before. The subject line was short: **"Think Bigger."**

He clicked.

◆◆◆

From: Nicole Langston
Subject: Think Bigger
Time: 11:17 PM
Attachment: "Beyond the Balance Sheet.pdf"

James,

I know yesterday got under your skin. That wasn't the intention, but it was necessary.

You've always believed in precision. In process. In measurable outcomes. I respect that–it's part of what makes you so damn good at what you do. But what if we could apply that same precision to the parts of planning we've never dared to quantify? Aging. Illness. Emotion. Time. What if we could see around corners–not just react when the road disappears?

That's where we're headed, whether we choose it or not. Clients are already there. The next generation won't tolerate ambiguity. They won't wait for annual reviews. They want insight in real time. And they want to feel like we know them, not just their money.

There's a system I've been piloting behind the scenes. It's not science fiction–it's already in play in firms just like ours. I've attached a brief.

You don't have to read it. Just... don't throw it in the same pile as the brochures.

You're not losing your compass, James. You're just re-aligning it.

–N

◆◆◆

He downloaded the file but didn't open it. Not yet.

Instead, James sat back, staring at the familiar landscape of his office. The calm, the quiet, the illusion of order. It had served him for so long. But now, he could feel the tremor in its foundation—a future approaching not in the form of chaos, but of complexity. Fast. Intelligent. Demanding.

Maybe Nicole was right. Maybe precision was no longer about defending the past.

Maybe it was about preparing for what the future would ask of them.

This wasn't a pivot. It was an inflection point.

The Whitmore children hadn't just challenged James's strategy—they had exposed its limitations. Nicole hadn't merely pitched a new model—she had offered a lifeline to relevance.

What came next wouldn't be a subtle shift in messaging or another quarterly report format. It would be foundational. Structural. Philosophical.

It was time to leave the harbor—and not just to weather the storms ahead, but to sail toward a horizon reshaped by algorithms, behavioral intelligence, and predictive planning tools: tools that didn't just map outcomes, but anticipated lives.

James didn't know it yet, but the path forward would begin with something unexpected. Not a whiteboard. Not a spreadsheet. A dashboard. An insight engine. A system that didn't just store data—it thought with you. The next chapter of the firm wouldn't be about managing money. It would be about mastering meaning.

CHAPTER 7

AI-The Intelligence That Watches Your Back

"AI is not about machines replacing humans. It's about machines augmenting what makes us human."

—Fei-Fei Li, AI pioneer and Stanford professor

Most advisors, including Nicole and James, proclaim their customers are their top priority, boasting mission statements built around trust and care. But the data tells another story. A recent J.D. Power study revealed that only 29% of customers believe their insurer simplifies complex policies. EY's global insurance outlook bluntly declared "historically low levels of customer trust."

There is, clearly, too often a disconnect between what advisors think and what clients experience. The solution? Ironically, it's something inherently nonhuman: technology.

Used well, AI and tech-enabled platforms can restore the human element—not by replacing empathy, but by enabling it. They give advisors more time, better insights, and more innovative tools to serve clients at the moments they need it most.

Nowhere was that clearer than in one quiet conversation between Nicole and James.

◆◆◆

James hovered near Nicole's desk, a folder tucked under his arm like a shield. Her dual monitors glowed with soft light, one displaying a client dashboard and the other a heat map of policy engagement across demographics.

"Your desk looks like NASA," he said, squinting at the graphics. "What are we launching?"

Nicole didn't turn around. "Trust," she said. "Or trying to. One touchpoint at a time."

James chuckled. "You sure that dashboard shouldn't come with its own advisory license?"

She gave a small smile. "I'm not asking it to give advice. I'm asking it to help me give better advice—to the right people, at the right time, using the method that reaches them."

He stepped closer. "You really believe all this digital wizardry can make us better at what we do?"

Nicole swiveled to face him, hands resting calmly on the desk. "James, you've said it yourself—we don't have enough time. Not enough hours in the day to meet every client where they are, in the way they prefer. Most of this industry still operates on texts, emails, and phone calls. That's fine for some, but it's not enough anymore."

"Technology can't care," he stated, his tone defensive but not unkind. "It can't look someone in the eye and say, 'I've got you.'"

"No," she said, "but it can make sure that we can! It can help us show up when it matters. It can pull up every relevant touchpoint for a client who's just had a baby or lost a spouse. It can track when someone's coverage is about to lapse, or when their plan no longer fits their family's needs or situation. Life's messy, things change. Better yet, it can free us from busywork so we can be present when empathy is needed most."

James was silent, mulling that over. He remembered just last month, missing a coverage review for a longtime client whose son had graduated. The reminder had been buried in a spreadsheet tab he hadn't opened.

"I just..." he started, unsure. "I worry we're trying to automate relationships."

"Not automate," Nicole said. "Enable. Think about it—Netflix tailors what you watch. Amazon knows what you'll reorder. Yet most carriers still send out the same generic letter to a 30-year-old entrepreneur and a 70-year-old widow. People don't feel seen. And trust erodes when people feel invisible."

He nodded slowly. "A recent Ernst & Young report said trust in insurance is at an all-time low."

"Because people associate complexity with opacity," she said. "And opacity with being misled. But technology can make complex plans easier to understand. Let's take, for example, a short or long-term care policy. It can simplify the application process, reduce claims friction, and keep us connected to clients in a way that feels human—if we design it right."

James glanced at her screen again. "So, this AI support system—what can it actually do?"

Turning back to her computer, Nicole clicked a few times and pulled up a client record. "Take Dan and Teresa. Early forties. Two kids. One mortgage. Used to communicate via email. The last couple of months, they stopped opening them. The AI tracked the behavior change and recommended a pivot to text messages instead. I switched, and within two hours, Teresa texted me back to schedule a call. Turns out Dan was recently diagnosed with something serious. It was time to discuss supplemental coverage and review finances."

He frowned and freely admitted, "I never would've caught that."

"Exactly. You care. You always have," Nicole said, turning towards James and pointing gently at him. "But now you can care with foresight. With context. This isn't about replacing our judgment—it's about expanding our reach."

James sat down across from her, his arms crossed but no longer guarded. "Okay. What's the catch?"

Her expression serious, Nicole dropped her voice a half octave, theatrically deadpan. "If we don't understand the good and the bad about incorporating AI, then we go the way of Blockbuster. Except we won't even get the honor of being featured in a nostalgia documentary. We'll just... disappear into the recycling bin with old brochures and fax coversheets."

James chuckled, though a hint of concern lingered—it was clear he was deep in thought. Really thinking.

Nicole sensed it. She could have said more—about large language models learning to write retirement strategies, or voicebots now trained to detect emotional stress in client calls. She could have mentioned the exponential curve AI was riding, and the fact that the tools they were using today might look like digital training wheels a year from now.

But she didn't. Not yet.

She softened. "This is just the beginning, James. The AI I'm using now? It's basic—helpful, but basic. What's coming... It's bigger. Faster. Smarter. But I don't want us jumping into the deep end when we haven't learned to swim in this new current. One stroke at a time."

◆◆◆

As James continued to mull over the greater use of AI that Nicole was suggesting, something shifted in him—not a complete embrace, but a loosening of the grip he'd kept on the past.

"Technology doesn't eliminate the human connection," Nicole continued, "it reinforces it. Empathy and efficiency aren't rivals—they're partners. And when aligned well, they complement each other, making each stronger.

James rubbed his jaw. "Do you think clients know what they want? Or are we supposed to guess?"

"They know what they want—they just don't always know how to ask for it. And that's where the data helps. It's not about being robotic. It's about using the information we already have -to dig into what's in their best interest, more personally, more proactively."

He looked over at her monitor again, eyes narrowing with curiosity instead of skepticism. "You think this could build trust with the multiple generations you keep mentioning, so we don't lose them?"

"I think it's the only way to even try. We live in a world where a client's rare free time is pulled in every direction—by family, especially multigenerational families, social obligations, and the nonstop buzz of notifications and noise. "It's not that people don't value financial guidance—they just don't want to chase it. They want it when and how it suits them. For insurers and advisors, the message is clear: adapt or get ignored. You must show up where your clients already are, whether that's a text at 6 p.m., a quick in-app chat, or a personalized report that can be quickly understood.

As James stood quietly, Nicole's words still reverberated in the silence, something primal stirred in him—not just curiosity, but apprehension. This wasn't about onboarding new software or updating workflows. It was about rethinking what it even meant to serve, to advise, to protect. Because the truth was, what Nicole had shown him—client segmentation, behavioral triggers, smart CRMs—was no longer the cutting edge. It was the runway. Behind it, engines were roaring.

Across the industry, bots were already being trained to "think": to analyze tone of voice, facial expressions, and emotional volatility; to predict not just market behavior, but human behavior. AI was no longer content to observe data—it was beginning to interpret desire. And soon, perhaps sooner than anyone expected, it would begin to anticipate need before even the client was aware of it.

Empathy was being reverse-engineered. Not replaced. Replicated. Refined.

And whether the profession was ready or not, that next wave had already made landfall.

In a world where trust is fractured, attention spans are shrinking, and consumers expect personalization without friction, this *wasn't* the future of the firm. That future had already passed. This—this moment right here—was history being rewritten in real time. And James finally understood they weren't preparing for what's coming. They were already behind.

CHAPTER 8

From Concept to Strategy: Crossing the Threshold

Building the Safety Net with AI Support: Preparing for Retirement's Realities

The machines were learning faster than anyone had expected. Nicole's dashboard—once a quiet novelty—was already outdated in some corners of the industry. Newer systems were parsing sentiment in real-time client calls. Others were simulating portfolio stress tests against climate scenarios and personalized health markers. AI was no longer just optimizing; it was beginning to anticipate, to shape the terrain before advisors had even stepped onto it.

It was awe-inspiring. And a little terrifying, and impossible to ignore.

Nicole had hinted at the future, but just the surface of what AI had already achieved. What struck James wasn't just the technology itself, but the velocity. She hadn't laid out a distant or even an imminent vision—she had cracked open a door to something already constantly accelerating. He wanted to do some research so he could understand if everything he thought was "far off" was already knocking at the door—fast, bold, and changing everything. Or was it all hype?

Before wrapping up the other day, Nicole had recommended a few reports. A paragraph from a recent one he'd read stayed with him. It didn't just spotlight breakthroughs—it framed a reckoning. One passage cut deep: "We are entering a new chapter in technology—one shaped by a generalization of AI. Today's proliferation of accessible and ever-present AI will drive new levels of autonomy all throughout the business, evolving the ability to reinvent with tech, data, and AI. It will bring nearly limitless possibilities for innovation and growth, but also challenge enterprises' confidence in systems and the way they think about trust. The rush of an AI race is undeniable."

Then there was the second—the one calling this era the *Binary Big Bang*. James could still see the line highlighted on his screen: "Organizations are entering a generation-defining moment of transition: the Binary Big Bang. When foundation models cracked the natural language barrier, they kickstarted a shift in our technology systems—how we design them, use them, and how they operate. We are now at the precipice of more abundance, abstraction, and autonomy in our technology systems than ever before, and the decisions enterprises make today will profoundly impact what they can achieve for the next decade."

What once felt theoretical now rang unmistakably personal. This wasn't about keeping up—it was about deciding whether to lead or be left behind. Trust wasn't just a challenge—it was a currency. And strategy wasn't optional—it was urgent.

Yet amid the swirl of foundation models, predictive analytics, and accelerating autonomy, James had arrived at a simple, grounding truth: all the technological brilliance in the world meant little if it didn't translate into real, human reassurance. Clients weren't asking for models—they were searching for meaning. They didn't need just predictions; they needed preparation.

It wasn't enough to marvel at what AI *could* do. Now, it was time to confront what it *couldn't.* The deeply personal concerns that no algorithm could shoulder alone—healthcare choices, the realities of longevity, and the quiet, unspoken fear of outliving one's own security. Because when clients sat across the table—worried about a parent's sudden diagnosis, uncertain about Medicare choices, or questioning whether their money would last—they didn't want a dashboard. They wanted a human. Someone who could look them in the eye and say, "You're not alone. We have a plan."

AI could detect patterns. It could simulate outcomes. But it couldn't feel the weight of a widow's silence. It couldn't read the pause before a client asked, "Will I be a burden to my kids?" Trust wasn't just a technical issue—it was a relational one. Built over time, tested in crisis, and earned through presence.

For all its brilliance, whether right or wrong, James believed that AI still lacked something critical: the ability to reassure. Not just inform, but steady. Not just calculate risk but carry it together.

James was still turning it over in his mind days later. The reports. The speed. The trust gap. And then, at dinner that evening, his friend, Ernesto — brilliant and driven —shared that he is currently knee-deep in a Cognitive AI project to create not just responsive interfaces but ones that are convincingly human. Ernesto brought up *Her*—the story of a man falling in love with an AI operating system. At the time, he'd dismissed it like the others—fascinating, sure, but still fiction. Now, it didn't seem so far-fetched. Ernesto was developing a Cognitive AI that wasn't just about better language or facial mimicry. It was about *emulation*—human tone, human reaction, even simulated empathy, and beyond.

That thought shook James more than he expected.

Could machines really replace that? *Should* they? The question haunted him for a moment, but then something settled. A clarity.

Yes, AI might eventually *sound* human. It might even *feel* human to some. It might be able to challenge a person's responses. Still, for now, many clients—especially those navigating the deeply personal terrain of aging, illness, or intergenerational planning—didn't want someone who simply sounded like them. They wanted someone who *reflected* them. Someone who had lived loss, or raised children, or faced uncertainty at 2 a.m. and didn't want just a glowing computer screen with a reassuring spreadsheet and a prayer.

Someone who knew not just the data, but the doubt.

He now understood why he needed to move from just spreadsheets to holistic planning. What great advisors bring is the mirror, not the machine. A reflection of experience. A relationship built on more than logic, and built on life.

Two Weeks Later...

James paused outside Nicole's office door, coffee in hand, the weight of those insights still pressing on him. He knocked.

"Come in," Nicole replied, not looking away from her screen.

James stepped inside, noticing her dual monitors, which were lit with client heat maps and engagement alerts. Nicole glanced over, mildly surprised but steady.

"Well, what brings you here?" she asked, glancing up.

He offered a small smile. "I've been looking at those reports—you know, the one calling it the 'Binary Big Bang,' and the autonomy framework. At first, I thought it was a buzz. But... It's happening. Fast."

Nicole leaned back. "It always was, just a few noticed."

James set his coffee down and met her gaze. "So, tell me—what have these AI agents been doing while I've been wrangling spreadsheets?"

She gestured to her screens. "One monitors email engagement and flags when a client goes silent, then suggests a text instead. Another watches for policy or health updates and sends alerts before we see the drop-offs. They remember our client context. They chain interactions so nothing is lost."

James frowned. "But can they care?"

Nicole's eyes softened. "They can't *feel* fear, grief, or hope. But they can give us time and insight so *we* can. If a widow is overwhelmed and leaves things unspoken, the agent alerts us to the shift. We step in with presence, not algorithms."

He exhaled, taking it in. "So, these tools help us do more of what matters—not less."

"Exactly," she echoed. "They're not replacements. They're the guardrails—so we can be the human anchors when it counts."

James looked at her screens again. "Then it's not just about being efficient. It's about being available."

Nicole smiled. "Being human, at scale."

James nodded. "Okay—let's build that safety net."

Answering the Call to Innovate

Pilot Couple #1: Facing the Unseen Risk

The firm's office hummed with its usual energy as James and Nicole prepared for their meeting with one of the *pilot couples*. Today's clients—a couple nearing retirement—had worked with James for years, trusting his steady hand. They expected the usual review: portfolio performance, growth projections, and a focus on returns. But today's conversation would be about much more than numbers.

James stood by the conference table, the familiar weight of the folder steadying his hands even as a quiet unease simmered beneath his composed exterior. The concepts he was about to present still felt foreign, like trying to navigate a map without landmarks. Yet beneath the doubt, a new determination stirred—a growing awareness of what was at stake, not just for his clients but for the legacy of the firm itself. Nicole, seated to his right, gave him a nod of quiet encouragement. She was ready to support him, but this was James's moment to lead.

As the couple settled into their chairs, James began as he always did—reviewing their portfolio's performance, highlighting strong returns and steady growth. The comfort of routine steadied his nerves. But as the conversation approached its familiar close, he paused. The weight of what came next pressed on him. It was time to shift the narrative.

"There's something else we need to consider," James began, his voice steady but deliberate. He glanced at Nicole before continuing. "We've always focused on maximizing returns, but there are other risks—costs—that can undermine even the best strategies. One of the biggest is the possibility of outliving your money or experiencing a diminished lifestyle. People are living longer, and that brings new challenges."

The couple exchanged uncertain glances. This wasn't what they'd expected. But James pressed on, aware that he was guiding them into unfamiliar terrain.

"Healthcare costs in retirement can be significant," he said, a sense of urgency creeping into his tone. "In the U.S., the average lifetime retirement healthcare expenses are rising, and there's a growing shortage of care professionals. Let me ask—what do you estimate your future healthcare costs might be?"

The husband hesitated, his brow knitting as he searched for an answer. "I don't know. Maybe... $2,500 a year?" His voice wavered slightly, as if even he wasn't convinced by the number. The words hung in the air, thin and uncertain, amplifying the quiet discomfort that now settled over the room. It was a stark reminder of how unprepared most people were for the unexamined costs of healthcare in pre- and post-retirement years. More than that, it underscored a pervasive truth: most people had no real sense of the financial burden healthcare would place on their retirement and investments.

James cleared his throat, his own discomfort flickering to the surface. He glanced at Nicole, then back at the couple. "It's a common assumption," he said gently, his tone meant to reassure. "Most people think their healthcare costs will be relatively minor, just routine check-ups and a few prescriptions. But the reality is far more complex—and expensive."

James slid a report across the table, his fingers tapping the paper lightly as he summarized. "According to recent research, seniors are spending an average of close to $6,800 per person annually on healthcare. And that number is likely to increase."

A muscle twitched in the husband's jaw as he shifted uncomfortably, his expression caught between frustration and quiet alarm. "We've worked hard to save, but... how do you even begin to account for something like that? The husband's voice was a bit unsteady; his concern was evident. "Nearly $7,000 per person, every year? And what if something serious happens? Wouldn't those costs skyrocket?"

Nicole met his gaze, her expression calm but resolute, her voice steady against the weight of the question. "They could. That $7,000 is just the baseline—a starting point. When something serious happens, costs can rise dramatically, which is why planning is so critical. It's no wonder that more than 60% of Baby Boomers say they fear outliving their money more than they fear death itself."

She paused, letting the gravity of her words settle before continuing. "But that fear isn't really about numbers, is it? It's about losing control over your choices, your independence, and your quality of life. That's what we want to help you safeguard."

A moment of silence followed as the couple absorbed the information, their expressions shifting from mild surprise to a mix of curiosity and concern.

The husband broke the quiet, his tone tinged with both apprehension and resolve. "So... what do we do? How do we even begin to plan for something like this?"

Nicole nodded, her calm demeanor reassuring. "That's the question we need to answer—together. It starts with a plan that not only grows your wealth but also protects it. The good news is, we can do that together." She paused, her tone softening as she leaned slightly forward. "You've already built a strong foundation through smart saving and investing. Now it's about ensuring that the foundation is ready to handle the unexpected. Together, we'll look at strategies tailored to your needs—ways to safeguard your retirement from healthcare surprises while preserving the lifestyle you've worked so hard to achieve."

James felt a surprising swell of confidence as Nicole's words settled over the room. This was uncharted territory, but for the first time, he didn't feel out of place leading the way. He leaned forward slightly, his own voice steady now. "What matters most is that we take this step now, before those costs become real. It's about exploring options to manage healthcare and other costs associated with aging and putting the necessary pieces in place so that when you need them, they're readily available. The key is to build a safety net, to ensure those costs don't erode the lifestyle you've worked so hard to maintain or become a burden to your family or friends."

The wife shifted uneasily, her hands clasping together as if trying to hold her worry in place. "Where do we even start?" she asked, her voice tinged with a mix of apprehension and hope. "How do we make sure we're ready for something like this? That we're not caught off guard?"

James's tone was steady, reassuring. "There are several tools available to help address these concerns—long-term care insurance, health savings accounts, insurance products that combine growth with security, and repositioning assets to cover extended care expenses. I'm not an expert in all these areas, but we'll bring in specialists who can provide you with the detailed information you need. I'll be here to help guide you through the options and make sure you fully understand how each choice aligns with your goals and risk tolerance. The important thing is that you're aware of these potential costs now so that we can plan effectively for them together."

The couple exchanged a look, their earlier concern slowly giving way to curiosity about their options. The husband nodded. "We've always trusted your advice, James. If there's a better way to prepare, we're ready to listen."

Nicole smiled, sensing a breakthrough. "That's the right approach. We want to help you prepare now, so you can retire without fear of running out of money. It's all about balance—growing your wealth while making sure you're protected against unexpected healthcare events or complications of longevity."

James rose from his chair, extending his hand with renewed confidence. His voice carried a charge of energy, underscoring the conviction behind his words. "You've done an excellent job growing your portfolio. Now let's apply that same diligence to protecting what you've built. We'll work together to ensure that no matter how long you live, we will have risk mitigation options in place so your money will be there for you when you need it most."

As the couple walked out, their quiet conversation carried a different energy—less uncertainty, more resolve. They were impressed by the depth of care James and Nicole had shown—concerned not just with growing their wealth, but with safeguarding their future. They still had questions, but the clarity James and Nicole had offered cut through their initial hesitation. It wasn't just about protecting their finances; it was about reclaiming additional control over their future.

Pilot Couple Two: Planning in Her Footsteps

The second couple arrived mid-afternoon. Married for twenty-seven years, their retirement date was in sight. They'd built their plan around stability—diligent saving, strong investment performance, and no real debt. But what they hadn't built was a strategy based on this couple's definition of legacy.

James began with his usual calm: charts, analysis, and confidence in their financial health. As the conversation transitioned into the healthcare portion of the agenda, he braced himself for the usual skepticism or surface-level curiosity.

Instead, something unexpected happened.

The wife—quiet until now—spoke, not by asking a question, but with a story.

"My mother passed from pancreatic cancer," she said. Her tone was soft but unwavering. "She chose the Whipple procedure. For her, it meant enduring what was essentially multiple surgeries in one—removing and reconnecting several organs. She spent nine days in the hospital, came home to a regimen of medications, dietary changes, and a new reality. It was a life-altering event that demanded immense resilience, and she bore it with quiet strength."

Nicole shifted slightly, sensing something deeper.

"She was fine until suddenly... she wasn't. That's how it can go with serious illnesses. It waits quietly, then takes loudly."

James's brow furrowed—not from confusion, but from concern. For so long, he had trusted that numbers were enough—because that's what the industry taught him. Today, he was hearing something different. When given the space, his clients didn't talk about markets or returns. They discussed family, health, and finding peace of mind. What they needed was holistic planning—real, human-centered guidance.

"She never cried in front of us. Never allowed fear to take over. When we visited and started to get emotional, she'd send us out into the garage, into another room. She didn't want us to see her fall apart. She was carrying us... even then."

Nicole leaned in. "That's... incredible," she said quietly.

"She made a decision," the woman continued. "To protect our memories of her. My children visited once, when she still looked like Nana. After that, she asked them not to come back. And she didn't want them at the funeral."

James blinked. "You honored that?"

"I did. Even though it broke me. I wanted them there. But she didn't want their memories to end in a hospital or a funeral parlor. She wanted them to remember visits to her home in Florida and beach walks. And now, that's exactly what they remember. My son still tells his kids about those visits to Florida—just him and his sister without us." She glanced towards her husband. "They went to the beach, explored sights, and swam in her pool. She was a terrible cook," she added with a fond smile, "but somehow, they loved her cooking anyway. Even now, they roll with laughter, remembering the meals she made. It wasn't about the food—it was about love."

Nicole's eyes shimmered.

"She never talked about legacy," the wife continued. "But she left one anyway. Not through money. Through her choices. Quiet, selfless choices."

The room was still.

James finally cleared his throat. "I had no idea," he said.

Nicole, leaning slightly forward, placed a hand gently on the table. "She was preparing you, even as she was saying goodbye. That's legacy. And now... you're trying to do the same."

The woman nodded. "I don't want my children to carry the burden—the physical, psychological, or financial costs—of watching me navigate an extended care need or cognitive decline. I want to protect them. Just like she did."

She looked at both James and Nicole with quiet intensity.

"If you can help us build a healthcare safety net—one that preserves not just our finances but our family's peace of mind—then that's the kind of planning we want to do." Her husband simply nodded his agreement and added, "We don't need guarantees. We need options. And we need to know we've done everything we can to protect our family, including our sisters and brothers, from the hardest parts."

Nicole met his gaze, her own voice steady. "That's exactly what we're here for."

The wife reached for her husband's hand. "We want that. We just didn't know how to begin."

James, still moved, leaned in. "Then let's start now. You've done the hard part—loving your family enough to think this far ahead. We'll help with the rest."

As the couple left, there was no doubt: this was now more than just financial planning. James had seen something new—a daughter trying to replicate the grace her mother had shown. A couple answering a call that he didn't even know existed until the conversation made space for it.

And Nicole? She saw the path forward more clearly than ever. The future of the firm wasn't rooted in charts or rates of return alone, though those still mattered. It was in earning enough trust for clients to share their stories and values, and using that to shape retirement plans grounded in what truly matters to them.

For James and Nicole, the meeting marked a turning point. The pilot project was no longer a concept on paper—it was a living, breathing strategy. They weren't just managing portfolios; they were managing lives, guiding clients through the complex intersection of lifestyle, health, and wealth. The path ahead was still uncharted, but for the first time, it felt achievable.

CHAPTER 9

Tests, Gaps, Allies, and Doubts

When Clarity Demands Change

The conversations with their pilot couples marked more than a meaningful shift in client engagement—they signaled the beginning of something larger. For years, James and Nicole had offered trusted financial guidance, rooted in the technical strength of portfolio design, tax strategies, and disciplined investment principles. But now, they could no longer unsee what had been uncovered: clients wanted more than performance—they wanted peace of mind. The future of the firm wouldn't be built solely on charts and rates of return. It would be built on trust, storytelling, and understanding what clients truly value, and designing retirement plans that reflect that.

This wasn't just a philosophical shift. It was a business decision. And it demanded a new strategy.

James and Nicole were standing at a professional crossroads. The awakening they experienced with their pilot couples had exposed more than emotional insight—it revealed a path forward. If they were going to meet the evolving needs of their clients, they would need to evolve their business in turn. That meant exploring growth intentionally. They began to identify four potential avenues to expand their firm's impact: organic growth, external expansion through partnerships, technological innovation, and strategic mergers or acquisitions. Each path offered different rewards and different risks. But one thing was clear: standing still was no longer an option.

The Gaps in Longevity Literacy

As James ventured further into holistic planning with his most receptive clients, he quickly encountered a steeper learning curve than he'd anticipated. Bringing healthcare costs and the complexities that come with aging into financial discussions opened a floodgate of questions. Clients who had once been satisfied with basic investment advice now sought answers to complex issues James had long avoided. "Do I need to apply for Medicare if I work beyond 65?" one client asked. Another, in his mid-forties, threw him off balance with, "Could you speak to my parents? They need to understand the difference between Medicare Advantage and Medicare Supplements." These were not routine inquiries—they were deeply personal, pushing James beyond the bounds of his expertise.

Each question felt like a pebble dropped into his carefully balanced scales, tilting them closer to disarray. Guiding clients through portfolio management had always been his fortress—a domain where his expertise was unshakable. But now, as the tangled worlds of lifespan, healthspan, and wealthspan planning collided, James felt cracks forming in his foundation. The once-clear boundaries of his role had blurred, leaving him grappling with an uneasy vulnerability he couldn't ignore.

Meanwhile, Nicole confronted her own set of challenges. Her younger clients—especially those in their 30s and 40s—grew increasingly anxious about the future of Social Security. One particularly worried client asked, "I keep hearing that Social Security might not be around when I retire. How do I replace that income if it's cut back?" At the same time, clients in their 50s and 60s expressed growing unease about the system's sustainability. Concerns about the realities of those paying into the fund, the slow growth of its reserves, and the increasing outflow of benefits due to longer lifespans and higher payouts painted a troubling picture for their retirement security. Nicole recognized that these worries were reshaping how clients across generations approached retirement planning, making proactive strategies more critical than ever.

She also understood these weren't fleeting anxieties—they were tectonic shifts in how clients viewed their future. Social Security, once a pillar of retirement security, had become a question mark. And in that growing uncertainty, Nicole saw something else: an opening.

Without even labeling it as such, she had begun to expand the firm's services organically. She wasn't chasing scale or revenue; she was answering the call of relevance. Her clients weren't just asking for help with investments—they were seeking clarity, reassurance, and guidance in areas no longer covered by conventional planning.

To meet that need, Nicole made a pivotal decision. She enrolled in the National Association of Registered Social Security Analysts' program. She earned her designation as a Registered Social Security Analyst (RSSA), equipping herself with the specialized knowledge her clients were seeking—but few advisors were equipped to provide.

With her RSSA designation, Nicole approached Social Security questions with newfound confidence and depth. She reassured clients that while no one could predict the program's future, it was unlikely to vanish entirely. Yet, she emphasized the importance of preparing for potential changes by diversifying income strategies.

Some clients discussed working part-time while receiving Social Security benefits. Nicole explained that, before full retirement age, earnings above certain thresholds could temporarily reduce benefits, but these reductions were not permanent. She reassured them that once they reached full retirement age, any withheld benefits would be restored.

Others were curious about spousal benefits. Nicole confidently outlined how a spouse could receive up to 50% of their partner's benefit if it exceeded their own, and she also clarified the mechanics of survivor benefits, helping clients understand how these provisions could provide stability after a partner's death.

Navigating pension-related questions also became second nature. Nicole broke down the intricate rules of the Windfall Elimination Provision (WEP) and the Government Pension Offset (GPO). These policies often blindsided retirees with pensions from jobs that didn't contribute to Social Security, reducing their expected payments. By addressing these potential pitfalls early, Nicole empowered her clients to make informed choices, sparing them from unwelcome surprises.

For couples, Nicole emphasized the crucial role of survivor benefits, often misunderstood and underutilized. Many retirees are confused about survivor benefits and spousal benefits, failing to plan effectively. She emphasized that survivor benefits could be claimed as early as age 60, prior to spousal benefits, and explained how survivors could strategically delay claiming one benefit to maximize the other. The most pressing cases, she noted, were when a spouse passed away young, leaving behind a surviving spouse with children. In these cases, survivor benefits were indispensable.

Nicole also delved into the complexities of the family maximum benefit, a limit on how much a family can collect based on one earner's work history. Families with younger spouses, minor children, or disabled children faced especially intricate claiming decisions. Nicole recognized that while software could help optimize these cases, a deep understanding of benefit rules was essential to guide families through the process.

These scenarios were just a sampling of the challenges Nicole addressed as an RSSA. Recognizing that the firm's clients would benefit from deep expertise and personalized guidance, Nicole spearheaded the creation of a dedicated Social Security/Retirement Planning (SSRP) team. She began by identifying talent within the firm—those with a knack for understanding complex systems and communicating them clearly. Through targeted training programs and client meetings, Nicole transformed this group into a specialized unit capable of addressing the increasingly complex questions that clients brought to the table.

In collaboration with her growing SSRP team, Nicole helped clients navigate issues such as Social Security Disability Insurance (SSDI), taxation of Social Security income, and planning considerations for self-employed business owners. By leveraging her certification and fostering a culture of shared knowledge, Nicole ensured the team demystified the complexities of maximizing lifetime Social Security benefits rather than focusing solely on annual or monthly optimizations.

A Model for Organic Growth: Proving the Concept

Nicole viewed the development of the Social Security/Retirement Planning (SSRP) Team as more than just a means to address a growing gap in client concerns—it was a proof of concept. She wanted James to see that organic growth within the firm wasn't just possible but essential. By leveraging internal talent, structured mentorship, and targeted expertise, she created a specialized unit that transformed how they addressed Social Security complexities.

From the outset, Nicole's leadership was hands-on, identifying promising team members, guiding their education, and ensuring they had the tools necessary to excel. The success of the SSRP Team was undeniable. Clients benefited from deeper, more personalized guidance, and the firm strengthened its reputation as a credible, trusted authority on Social Security strategy.

However, Nicole also recognized a crucial reality: future expansion couldn't depend on her direct personal involvement. This model had to become a replicable framework—one that could be applied to other specialized areas without requiring her constant oversight. She understood that the firm's longevity and scalability depended on fostering a culture where expertise could grow organically, led by those within the firm who were willing to step up and take the lead.

With the SSRP Team as a blueprint, Nicole began strategizing ways to encourage similar initiatives in other critical areas. The foundation had been laid. Now, it was about embedding this philosophy into the firm's DNA, ensuring that future teams could develop and thrive without waiting for a single leader to drive every new initiative.

Nicole had proven that organic growth wasn't just a concept—it was a sustainable path forward. The challenge now was ensuring it became a standard practice, seamlessly integrated into the firm's evolution.

Confronting Unaddressed Risks and Staying Compliant

As James and Nicole fielded increasingly complex questions, they both acknowledged that their clients' needs were evolving. The days when basic investment advice sufficed are long gone. Today's clients demand comprehensive, holistic planning. From healthcare to Social Security, from government programs to insurance, taxes to legacy and business planning, the range of concerns was broadening. As James and Nicole delved deeper into these topics, they recognized that to serve their clients better, it was essential to remain compliant with ever-evolving regulations.

One afternoon, after a particularly intense meeting, James leaned against Nicole's office doorframe, his expression more contemplative than usual. The slanting rays of the late afternoon sun filtered through the blinds, casting lines of light and shadow across the room, softening the day's sharp edges.

"I didn't think embracing holistic planning would shift the conversations this much, this fast," he admitted, unease creeping into his voice. "We're diving into areas I'm not comfortable with—healthcare costs, the complications of longevity, Medicare options, insurance, long-term care, and now, crisis planning. And with these new regulatory proposals on the horizon, we've got to be even more careful."

Nicole looked up from her laptop and nodded in agreement. "I've noticed the same thing. Clients are asking about everything—caregiving support, annuities, life insurance, even taxes. It's like they're bracing for a world where they must take even more control over their retirement. It validates what I've been saying all along—retirement planning isn't just about investment returns anymore. It's about anticipating clients' needs before they even realize they have them."

With her characteristic wit softened by understanding, Nicole smiled. "Welcome to the new frontier, James. We've opened Pandora's box, but I don't think we're in over our heads. We just need to be strategic—figure out what we can manage in-house and where we need to bring in specialists. We can no longer afford to react. We need to lead."

The faint murmur of the office beyond her door whispered of steady activity, a reminder of the world continuing outside their conversation. James had always feared stretching themselves too thin. They couldn't be everything to everyone. What they needed now were specialists, fresh perspectives, and younger talent to bridge the gap between their established practice and the rapidly shifting landscape.

James absorbed her words thoughtfully. "You're right. We've always prided ourselves on being experts, but now we need to become learners again. Let's schedule a strategy session and figure out how we want to adapt. If we're going to meet these new expectations—and stay compliant—we need a plan that's sustainable for us and valuable for our clients."

The tension had shifted. It wasn't about old versus new anymore—it was about acknowledging that retirement planning and wealth management had become far more complex than they had anticipated. But despite the discomfort, James felt a flicker of resolve. The deeper their conversations with clients became, the clearer it was that adaptation wasn't just a choice—it was essential.

As James walked back to his office, his footsteps echoed against the polished floor, each one a steady beat in the quiet uncertainty of what lay ahead. The upcoming strategy session with Nicole would be crucial.

They needed to figure out how to leverage their strengths—and where they would need to rely on others.

◆◆◆

Facing Pushback

Not all clients were on board with the broader planning approach, a reality James encountered head-on with Mr. Holloway. A no-nonsense businessman in his late 60s, Mr. Holloway had built his career on decisiveness and efficiency—traits he expected from those who managed his wealth. After their usual review of portfolio returns, James cautiously steered the conversation toward potential health-related costs and their impact on Mr. Holloway's long-term goals. He framed the discussion in terms of legacy, ensuring that the wealth Mr. Holloway had worked so hard to accumulate could support his grandchildren's education or help them launch their own businesses.

At first, Mr. Holloway listened, his sharp eyes betraying no reaction. But as James broached the topic of planning for longevity and any associated healthcare expenses, his expression hardened.

"James, I get where you're coming from," Mr. Holloway interrupted, his tone clipped. "But I've already got a team for that. My focus with you is growth—plain and simple. Let's stick to the returns and make sure that legacy stays intact."

The finality in his voice left no room for rebuttal. James nodded, swallowing his slip-up as Mr. Holloway rose to leave. "Of course," he replied evenly, his professional composure masking the nagging unease creeping into his thoughts.

As the door closed behind Mr. Holloway, James sank back into his chair, his mind racing. Had Mr. Holloway misunderstood his intentions? Or worse—had he assumed James was merely angling for more business? It wasn't an unreasonable conclusion. After all, for years their relationship had been defined by numbers: portfolio growth, returns, risk management.

The shift toward holistic planning was new, untested, and, from a client's perspective, potentially self-serving. If James's message wasn't clear, if a cohesive strategy didn't support it, it could easily be misconstrued as little more than an attempt to pad the firm's offerings.

When James relayed the conversation to Nicole later that afternoon, her reaction was swift. "This is exactly why we need a unified strategy," she said, her tone sharp but not unkind. "Clients like Holloway have fragmented teams because they don't see us as the one-stop solution. We're part of the equation, but we're not the whole answer—and that's a risk."

James frowned, the weight of her words settling heavily. He hadn't thought of it that way. But she was right. While their pilot initiative had made strides, the lack of a comprehensive approach left clients like Mr. Holloway vulnerable to conflicting advice and fragmented plans. For the firm to truly lead, it couldn't just dabble in holistic planning—it had to own it, integrate it, and present it as a seamless extension of its core services.

"We can't afford to let others fill in the gaps for our clients," Nicole continued, her voice steady but resolute. "If we don't offer the full picture, we are letting clients down, and someone else will fill the gap. And when that happens, we'll lose their trust entirely."

James exhaled slowly, his mind already churning with ideas. It was clear they couldn't afford to treat holistic planning as an optional add-on. It needed to be positioned as an indispensable part of their service—a strategy woven into the very fabric of what they offered. And it needed to be presented with the same confidence and clarity as their investment expertise.

"We need to show clients like Holloway that it's all connected," Nicole said, her voice quieter now but no less determined. "Growth, legacy, healthcare—it's all part of the same story. If we don't connect those dots for them, someone else will."

James nodded, his eyes alight with the energy of a new challenge—even if his words carried more certainty than he truly felt. "Exactly," he said, more to anchor himself than to persuade. The vision was clear—but how to get there, less so. "The first step is getting our team aligned. Everyone needs to be on the same page, delivering the same message. No more gaps. No more fragmentation. If we're going to do this, we're going to do it right."

CHAPTER 10

Steady Approach to Realization

Lighter Moments with Heavy Undertones

Once again, James and Nicole sat in the familiar conference room—the same place where their initial discussions about client satisfaction and expansion had sparked the deeper conversations that led them to this moment. But today, the atmosphere felt heavier, more saturated with the weight of impending decisions.

"Alright, James, let's get down to business," Nicole said, sliding a brightly colored agenda across the table with a grin that carried just enough levity to lighten the mood. "No doomsday predictions today—just a bit of strategic brainstorming. Think jazz, not opera. We're talking subtle improvisation, not a full-scale production."

James allowed himself a chuckle, but his smile faded as his eyes scanned the agenda. "You've got a talent for making this sound easy, Nicole. But this isn't just another brainstorming session. It feels… pivotal. Like one wrong step, and we lose more than just our footing."

Nicole settled back in her chair, crossing one leg over the other as she spoke with measured calm. "Yes, I get that! But you know the saying—if you're not growing, you're shrinking—or worse—fossilizing. And I refuse to become a relic. Let's start with a phased rollout, test a few new services, and see what sticks," Nicole said. "No need for a midlife crisis makeover. Clients aren't just looking for growth anymore; they're looking for stability in the face of uncertainty. They're looking for expertise with empathy. That's what we're helping them tackle. We're not adding confusion—we're adding clarity to the questions they didn't even realize they needed to ask."

She paused before continuing, her tone measured but firm. "And part of that clarity might come from outside voices. We can't assume we have to build everything from scratch. Sometimes growth doesn't mean doing more ourselves—it means bringing in strategic partners or consultants who can expand what we offer without diluting who we are."

James nodded slowly, the weight of the decision settling on him like a tangible force. "I'm on board with testing the waters. We've learned a lot from the Client Pilot Program and the success of the SSRP Team. But bringing in outside consultants or partners?" He hesitated. "That feels risky. It's like inviting a third wheel onto our perfectly balanced tandem bike. What if we lose control of what's made us successful?"

Nicole softened her tone, but her conviction remained firm. "I hear you, James. But think of it this way—if we keep peddling the same way without adjusting to the terrain, we're bound to hit a pothole or two. And let's be honest—no one looks good flying over the handlebars."

James couldn't help but chuckle. "Alright, fair point. But we still need to be careful. If we stretch ourselves too thin, it's not growth—it's collapse."

Nicole's expression grew more serious, though her characteristic smile lingered. "Absolutely. We'll take it slow, be strategic, and make sure our growth is more like a graceful evolution than a sudden overhaul. We don't need to tackle everything at once. Maybe we could start by bringing in a specialist for healthcare, Medicare, or caregiving trends on a project basis. We can dip our toes in without diving headfirst. Nicole smiled gently. "What if we find someone who can help us go farther than we ever could alone?"

James felt some of the tension in his shoulders ease. Nicole's blend of humor and practicality had always grounded him. "I'm feeling better about this. Let's draft a framework for thoughtful, incremental growth. No need to rush—just make sure we're heading in the right direction."

Nicole's eyes sparkled with satisfaction. "Perfect! I think we're steering this ship in the right direction. And don't worry—we can add floaties if you need them. Let's keep it smart, keep it *us*, and, most importantly, let's keep it fun. Who says planning can't have a little flair?"

James placed a dramatic hand over his heart, his expression comically grave. "Me? With flair? Unthinkable! Next thing you know, I'll be wearing patterned socks and using emojis in emails."

Nicole burst into laughter, her genuine delight filling the room. As they wrapped up, James felt they had struck the right balance between serious strategy and Nicole's much-needed levity. The risks were real, but if they approached this expansion with the same clarity and personal attention that had built their firm, they would be in good shape.

As James gathered his notes and left the conference room, he felt lighter, more optimistic. They were venturing into new territory, but with Nicole's sharp insight and their shared focus, he was confident they could navigate this transition without losing what made their firm special. The path ahead would undoubtedly have its challenges, but for the first time, James felt truly ready to face them—together.

◆◆◆

The Ordeal

Then it happened—the email that sent James spiraling. James sat frozen, the glow of the screen casting harsh shadows across his face. The words blurred as his mind raced, replaying the client's blunt message on an unrelenting loop. Each sentence cut deeper, a harsh indictment of the very direction he'd started to believe in. One of his longest-standing clients—someone who had been with him since the firm's early days—had sent a curt, direct message: he was taking their business elsewhere.

"I don't recognize the firm anymore, James. You're pushing us into areas we never signed up for. This isn't what we came to you for. If you'd done your job right, these concerns wouldn't even be on our radar. We're moving our account elsewhere. Halloway."

That was it. No complaints, no specific grievances—just a polished farewell from a longtime client James had considered all but permanent. A fixture. A given.

The rational side of him knew that losing clients was part of the business. People's needs changed, and circumstances evolved. But this wasn't just any client. It was one of his earliest, the kind he'd built trust with over years of careful portfolio management. And now, he was gone.

The loss was regrettable but an inevitable part of running a firm. But instead, for James, it reopened something he thought he had buried—the irritating doubts left behind by Mr. Halloway's abrupt reaction weeks earlier. Halloway's frustration over the firm's expanding focus on holistic planning had stung at the time, but James had convinced himself it was an isolated case. A man resistant to change who might come around. Nothing more.

Now, he wasn't so sure.

What if they *had* pushed too hard? What if he *had* miscalculated how willing certain clients were to engage in deeper conversations about health and longevity? What if more clients felt the same way but hadn't said it out loud yet?

He exhaled sharply, his fingers drumming against the desk. He hated this feeling—the creeping second-guessing, the way one setback had the power to unravel months of confidence. The firm *was* evolving, and he had believed in that evolution. But now? Now he wasn't sure if he had the conviction to see it through.

The sound of footsteps pulled him from his spiral. Nicole walked into his office, pausing just long enough to assess the tension in his posture.

His usual sharp focus was absent; instead, his eyes were fixed on the screen, his expression unreadable.

"James?" Her voice was careful, controlled.

He didn't turn right away, his jaw tightening before he finally exhaled and leaned back in his chair. "I lost a very good client today," he said, his voice flatter than he intended.

Nicole didn't react immediately, waiting for him to continue.

"Not just any client. A longtime one. No complaints, no conversation—just an email saying they're moving on. And I can't shake the feeling that Halloway may be one of many."

Nicole frowned, stepping closer. "Halloway?"

James let out a short, humorless laugh. "Yeah. I thought I'd put that one to rest, but this email dragged it right back up. What if we're wrong, Nicole? What if we're pushing people in ways that don't feel right or comfortable to them? We built this firm on trust, and now I'm wondering if I'm risking that trust by introducing changes that might feel out of step—or even invasive—for some of our clients."

Nicole studied him, then pulled out a chair and sat across from him, folding her arms, elbows on the desk. "James, losing a client stings—I get it. And yeah, Halloway wasn't exactly subtle in his pushback. But you're connecting dots that aren't there. This isn't about one decision unraveling everything we've built."

James shook his head. "Then why does it feel like it is?"

Nicole leaned forward. "Because you're in it. Because change is uncomfortable. And because you're the kind of person who sees one step backward and forgets about the ten steps forward. You think that email and Halloway's reaction define the entire direction of this firm? "A recent Lincoln Financial Group survey that I put on your desk showed that medical and long-term care expenses are seen as bigger threats to retirement portfolios than inflation or even the economy. We're helping our clients stay ahead of those threats. So, let's look at the clients who *do* get it. The ones who tell us they finally feel heard, the ones who leave meetings saying, 'I wish I'd known this sooner.' Those are the people who are proving this works."

James exhaled slowly, pressing his fingers to his temple as if trying to hold back a rising doubt. "It's just hard not to let doubt creep in."

She let the silence breathe for a moment before continuing.

"And for what it's worth, Halloway didn't have to leave. You never forced the issue—you backed off, you never gave him an ultimatum. If he walked away, or in his case marched off, maybe it wasn't because you pushed too hard. Maybe it was because he wasn't ready to face some concerns or issues that your question seemed to touch on. Maybe he wasn't ready to move forward, so he ran."

James said nothing at first. Her words settled in like a slow-falling weight, not heavy with accusation, but with truth. He hadn't considered that before—that Halloway's departure might have had less to do with disruption, and more to do with discomfort. Not everyone was ready to grow. Not everyone could.

He drew in a quiet breath, more to steady his thoughts than to find answers. "Maybe," he said, almost to himself.

She let the silence sit for a moment before continuing. "If a client leaves, that's their choice. But we're not going to let one departure—or even a few—define our success. We're making an impact, James. And the right clients? The ones who see the value in what we're doing. They're the ones who will stay."

James stared at her for a long moment before finally nodding. "Yeah," he murmured. "Yeah, maybe you're right."

Nicole smirked. "Not maybe. I *am* right."

The corner of his mouth lifted slightly, the first hint of a real expression he'd shown since she walked in. "Let's not get carried away."

She grinned, standing and straightening her blazer. "Good. Now, let's stop brooding over one email and focus on the clients who *are* here."

James exhaled, shaking off the last traces of doubt. "Alright. OK."

And just like that, the weight that had threatened to settle in his chest lightened—just enough.

CHAPTER 11

The Multigenerational Impact of Longevity

A few weeks later, the tone between James and Nicole had changed. James's resistance had softened, though traces of unease lingered, particularly when their discussions veered into the delicate terrain of future care planning—a subject fraught with emotional and practical complexities. As they settled into their familiar spot in the conference room—their unofficial space for tough conversations and pivotal decisions—James was the first to speak.

"I've been thinking about where we are taking the firm—about how future care planning needs to become part of our core strategy. I see the value, but it's a tough conversation. People don't always like talking about 'that' part of their future. Some even have trouble finding the right words, and some haven't fully sorted out their own thoughts."

Nicole nodded thoughtfully. "You're right. Future care planning isn't an easy conversation, but delaying it only makes it harder. In *How Not to Pull*

Your Life Apart Caregiving, the author illustrates, through real stories, how avoidance leads to crisis, while early discussions pave the way for dignity, financial stability, and family harmony. The reality is most people don't recognize how crucial these conversations are—until they're forced into them."

James leaned back, exhaling as he tapped his fingers on the table. "That's the problem, isn't it? Acknowledging the need is one thing, but actually confronting it? That's another story. People don't want to think about aging, let alone losing their independence or paying for help."

Nicole folded her hands, her voice measured but firm. "And that's why we need to shift the way we present it. The book makes a powerful point—this isn't about fear. It's about freedom. When people take control of their care plans early, they're not just avoiding a crisis; they're ensuring they get to live on their own terms, in the way they choose, without placing a heavy burden on anyone else."

James nodded slowly, the logic settling in. "So, the key isn't to push—it's to reframe. We don't talk about decline. We talk about choices. We show them how planning now protects what they've built and keeps them in charge of their future."

"Exactly," Nicole agreed. "But it takes patience. It's not a single conversation—it's a journey. The book illustrates how various families navigated these discussions, what approaches were effective, and which were not. Some needed small, gradual steps. Others needed a wake-up call. But in every case, planning led to peace of mind."

James was quiet for a moment, clearly thinking it through. "It's a tough sell, but I see it now. Suppose we can help them past their initial resistance. In that case, we're not just saving them from financial and emotional turmoil—we're giving them the opportunity to live longer, healthier, and more secure lives."

Nicole smiled, sensing the shift in his thinking. "That's exactly it, James. This isn't just about preparing for what *might* happen. It's about ensuring they can fully enjoy what *will* happen. It's worth the effort. That's the kind of value that sets us apart."

James sat up straighter, the tension in his shoulders easing. "Alright. Let's do it. Let's start weaving these conversations into our strategy. If we do this right, not only will we help our clients—we'll deepen their trust in us."

Nicole's logic was clear, but the client's words lingered in the back of his mind, a constant hum of warning. The path forward wasn't without risk, but retreating now would mean abandoning everything they'd worked to build.

"Alright," he said finally. "We keep moving forward, but we tread carefully. We'll adjust where we need to, but we don't turn back."

Nicole's smile held both relief and determination. "Exactly. It's about refining, not retreating. We're not here to complicate things—we're here to help clients anticipate challenges before they become crises. Clients are trusting us to help them navigate, even if they don't fully understand the journey yet."

◆◆◆

Recognizing Red Flags in Client's Plans

A couple of days later, as Nicole drove back from a client meeting, the conversation replayed in her mind, each detail etched vividly in her memory. On the surface, the meeting had gone well—perhaps too well. The couple she'd met with had been poised, articulate, and deeply engaged. Yet, beneath their composed words, Nicole detected the subtle tremors of vulnerability. To her surprise, another "pilot client" seemed to have emerged. They seemed to not only grasp the invisible threats she had delicately revealed but now had a clear understanding of unspoken risks threatening to unravel their carefully crafted retirement plan.

The couple had spoken at length about caring for the wife's aging parents. Though they described the situation calmly, Nicole heard the exhaustion woven into every phrase. It lingered in their voices, their pauses, their eyes. Caregiving had taken its toll—not just physically, but emotionally and financially. The wife's father, once a paragon of financial prudence, now found himself adrift, his savings devoured by mounting medical bills, part-time caregiving costs, and inflation. The burden had quietly shifted to his daughter and son-in-law, who were quietly funneling their own resources to fill the widening gap.

For a time, they had managed. But Nicole could sense their mounting anxiety, an unspoken question hanging heavy in the room: *What if we can't keep this up, and what effect will it have on our own retirement plan?* The burden of caregiving had begun to overshadow their own future. They were resolute in their desire to shield their children from a similar fate, but despite their determination, they couldn't see a clear way forward.

As Nicole navigated the familiar stretch of road, unease settled over her—the weight of their story pressing in. This wasn't just a financial challenge; it was a deeply human vulnerability; a quiet plea embedded in their words. They were caught in what's often called the "sandwich generation." She'd read recently that it's now being dubbed the "Panini generation"—pressed on all sides.

It wasn't just about preserving assets; it was about preserving dignity—ensuring her clients, their aging parents, and often their children could navigate the complexities of aging and caregiving without losing themselves in the process. How do you safeguard a sense of identity when the future is rife with uncertainties? Given their experience with the wife's parent, the fear of becoming both caretaker and, inevitably, the cared-for loomed large, casting long shadows over their lives and those of their children.

Recognizing Red Flags in the Firm's Plan

Her thoughts drifted inward as the miles slipped by. She and James had spent years urging clients to prepare—to put a retirement plan in place, to get everything in writing. Yet here they were, navigating the unknown without their own playbook. The irony struck sharply. They had collected enough pilot cases to understand one irrefutable truth: a cookie-cutter approach wouldn't suffice. Every client's story was unique, demanding a flexible but solid strategy. It was time to stop dancing around the edges of their own practice and lives. They needed something concrete—a framework, a vision that could guide not only their clients but themselves through the fog of uncertainty, toward a place of stability, credibility, and clarity.

The Hardest Plan to Write

James had arrived early at the office, drawn by the comfort of routine and the quiet focus of reviewing client portfolios—still his favorite part of the work. When he finished, the ticking wall clock filled the silence, each measured beat a reminder of the one resource they couldn't manage: time. James sat at his desk, his neatly arranged folders and reports providing a sense of order that usually calmed him. Today, though, those precise columns of numbers felt hollow, like a fortress built on a foundation that was starting to shift beneath him. He could feel the pressure to evolve—but no clear path had yet revealed itself. The shape of the future remained frustratingly vague, and for the first time in a long time, James wasn't sure what the next move should be.

The sharp staccato of Nicole's heels echoed down the hallway, cutting through the quiet. Her stride was brisk, her energy carrying an intensity that James immediately picked up on. She swept into the room with her characteristic flair, but there was no trace of her usual light-hearted banter. Her expression was focused, her movements purposeful.

"Well, don't just sit there," she said, half-teasing but entirely serious. "We need to talk."

James looked puzzled, momentarily caught off guard. "Should I be worried or relieved?" he asked, leaning back in his chair, trying to gauge her mood.

Nicole's lips curved into a small smile, but the weight behind her gaze remained intense.

"Relieved for now," she quipped, her voice a playful mix of dry wit and pointed urgency, like a comedian setting up the punchline to a truth no one wanted to hear. "But let's be honest, James—it's embarrassing. Every day, we tell our clients how crucial it is to have a clear, written plan, and here we are... winging it."

James's lips curved into a wry smile. "You know," he said slowly, "I've been thinking the same thing. We've been so focused on reacting to our clients' needs, we've completely neglected our own strategy."

Neither of them spoke, a quiet moment where nothing needed to be said. The realization had been building for weeks, maybe months, but now it was impossible to ignore. They couldn't keep putting off the inevitable. The time for hesitation had passed.

"We need to fix this," Nicole said, her voice resolute. "No more improvising. No more waiting. No more pilot clients. If we're going to guide our clients through their storms, we need to make sure our own ship is seaworthy."

James nodded, his own resolve settling in. "Agreed. Let's block out this weekend. No interruptions. Just us, a whiteboard, and a plan we can believe in."

Nicole raised an eyebrow. "A weekend? Your wife's going to love that."

James smiled. "Actually, she might be relieved. She said I've seemed... off lately. Said it's not like me to be this unsettled." He shook his head. "And she's right. I've always been the steady one—the numbers guy. But lately, the numbers haven't been enough."

Nicole softened. "That's because this isn't just about numbers anymore—and we don't have a written plan. Nothing we can run the math on, test, or truly measure. It's all still too abstract."

James nodded again, more slowly this time. "Exactly. That's why we need the weekend. I need something solid to stand on again."

Their eyes met, a shared determination passing between them. They had decided on an updated strategy to help clients prepare for contingencies, guiding them through the uncertainties of aging, finances, and family dynamics. But now it was their turn to do the work—to build a framework that could carry their firm, and themselves, into the future.

PART II

Step-by-Step Strategic Growth Framework

CHAPTER 12

From Concept to Strategy

Mapping Out Core Components

That weekend, Nicole and James dove headfirst into Stephen Covey's principles, letting his timeless wisdom guide their path. For years, they had preached clarity and purpose to their clients—yet their own firm had been operating on instinct, a handful of pilot cases, and an organic growth path that lacked a clear, intentional strategy. The time for improvisation was over. They were ready to chart a course grounded in precision, alignment, and conviction.

Covey's first principle—*Start with the End in Mind*—sets the tone. They envisioned their firm three to five years into the future: not just financially stronger, but purpose-driven. A leader in holistic retirement planning that addresses the complexities of multigenerational wealth, long life expectancies, and caregiving challenges. Growth wasn't about empire—it was about legacy.

But clarity didn't come from vision alone. To shape their ambition into an actionable direction, they returned to the firm's newly drafted

Manifesto, a 12-point declaration they had worked through line by line the week prior. Each tenet had forced difficult but necessary conversations. At times, they debated with the edge of conviction that only long-time partners could survive. But by Sunday evening, they weren't just aligned—they were galvanized.

Together, they recommitted to:

1. **Start with empathy.** Every client story begins with understanding, not assumptions.
2. **Lead with purpose, not just performance.** Financial growth is only meaningful when it aligns with a client's deeper life goals.
3. **Respect the legacy while guiding innovation.** Embrace new tools and strategies without abandoning foundational wisdom.
4. **Anticipate life's unpredictability.** Plan not just for markets, but for real lives.
5. **Empower multigenerational families.** Retirement planning is no longer an individual endeavor—it's a generational one.
6. **Create frameworks, not formulas.** Every plan should be adaptable, resilient, and reflective of a client's life and values.
7. **Build bridges between wealth and health.** Recognize that financial longevity is inextricably tied to physical and emotional well-being.
8. **Honor trust above all.** Clients don't need more information—they need a trusted interpreter.
9. **Stay curious, not complacent.** What worked yesterday may not be enough for tomorrow.
10. **Invest in conversations.** The real value lies in listening, asking, and understanding before taking action.
11. **Plan for transitions, not just end goals.** Life isn't a single endpoint—it's a series of thresholds.
12. **Protect the dignity of aging.** Planning should never reduce people to liabilities. It should elevate their humanity.

◆◆◆

Covey's second principle—*Align Enhancements with Core Values*—resonated even more deeply after they solidified their manifesto. They knew that growth for its own sake could erode the trust they had spent years nurturing. Every service, hire, or expansion had to reflect what they now saw as their true north: integrity, foresight, emotional intelligence, credibility, and advocacy for the whole client, not just their net worth.

With those principles and their manifesto as a compass, they mapped two distinct paths forward:

1. **Organic Expansion** – Hire in-house specialists to deepen expertise under one roof, using the success of the SSRP (Social Security Retirement Planning) Team as a foundational model.
2. **External Expansion through Strategic Partnerships** – Build a trusted network of professionals, including Medicare experts, elder law attorneys, and long-term care planners, to seamlessly complement their services.

Each path had merit. Each required diligence. But what mattered most was that both aligned with the newly articulated mission: to become architects of security, not just stewards of wealth.

As Sunday evening's amber light dimmed across the room, James and Nicole sat back, surveying the whiteboard now covered with notes, diagrams, and timelines. For the first time in a long time, they felt not just in control, but committed and settled. This wasn't yet a plan. It was a promise. A line drawn in the sand. Not just to their clients, but to each other.

The Strategy Won't Build Itself

A few weeks later, under the crisp light of a bright morning, Nicole leaned casually against James's desk, her playful energy back in full force. "Let's not become our own worst client," she teased, wagging a finger. "We decided to do this weeks ago. It just took us this long to take the next step—because, like our clients, we let 'busy' get in the way."

James gave a knowing nod, already anticipating where the conversation was headed

James grinned, fully aware she was right. "Fine. What's the game plan, boss?"

"We can't just choose blindly," she added, her tone shifting slightly. "Between the pilot program and the SSRP team, we've seen what organic growth can look like."

She paused, her tone turning more focused.

"Now it's about making the next strategic call: do we keep growing organically, or is it time to explore external expansion? We need to evaluate both—financially and from a personnel standpoint—to see what's truly sustainable."

Nicole's smile softened, her voice turning serious. "I'll focus on client experience—refining our communications, enhancing the practical steps, and ensuring seamless execution. You handle the numbers, projections, and logistics. We'll test both approaches and determine the best approach for each one."

"Deal," James said, nodding as he jotted down some notes. This wasn't just a pilot program anymore. It was a strategy—and they were committed to it.

◆◆◆

From Planning to Execution

They met in their usual spot in the conference room, but this time the energy was palpable. Notes from their weekend session had been refined into a detailed plan. What had started as scattered ideas about growth had crystallized into a living strategy—a playbook that would guide their growth. Today was about taking the next step: committing to execution.

Nicole stood by the screen, advancing through a clean, focused presentation that laid out their immediate priorities:

- **Phase 1:** Continue offering the expanded services with select clients, deepening their approach to longevity and multigenerational planning.

- **Phase 2:** Measure outcomes and refine the process, using real client and financial feedback to sharpen delivery and define best practices.
- **Phase 3:** Scale strategically—either by bringing on new talent or formalizing partnerships that align with their mission.

This wasn't a theory anymore. It was the blueprint for what came next.

As they moved forward with the plan, James reviewed the financial projections and staffing implications, his mind alive with both possibilities and risks.

"The numbers hold," he said, setting the papers down with measured confidence. "If we stay disciplined, we can grow without losing what makes us, well, us!"

Nicole nodded. "Good. Then let's get started. We've spent enough time philosophizing and testing the water with pilots—now we build."

Both partners were ready. Their iPads and laptops were filled with notes, spreadsheets, and insights from their exploration of Stephen Covey's principles of clarity, purpose, and alignment. The vision was clear, but now it was time to transform that vision into practical steps and set their plans into motion. Time to create the roadmap.

Nicole, ever the instigator, broke the silence. "Alright, let's get tactical," she said, her voice brisk and energized. "We've mapped out two distinct pathways for growth, but staying conceptual won't cut it anymore. It's time to break this down."

James nodded, flipping open his iPad and bringing up his meticulously organized notes. "We've agreed that Covey's principles will anchor our approach, and we're aligned on where we want to be in three to five years. Now it's about prioritizing. What's first? What resources do we need? And what can't wait?"

Nicole moved through her presentation, starting with a quick recap. "We agreed to flesh out the two pathways: expanding internally with new hires or building a network of trusted partners. We agreed not just to choose blindly, but to evaluate both in terms of immediate client impact and long-term scalability."

James adjusted his glasses, scanning the financial breakdowns he'd prepared. "For in-house growth, the upfront investment is higher—salaries, onboarding, benefits—but it gives us full control over service delivery, which aligns with our values: consistency and personalization."

He paused, his gaze settling on the data drawn from the Social Security and Retirement Planning (SSRP) team that Nicole had built during the pilot phase. "The SSRP team gives us a solid foundation to analyze the numbers. The feedback we've received so far—client retention rates and satisfaction scores—proves that having in-house expertise creates a stronger bond and solid credibility with our clients. It's clear they value the seamless experience."

Nicole pressed her lips together in thought before responding. "Exactly. That's one of the biggest arguments for growing internally. But we also need to be realistic about capacity. Even with the SSRP team's success, we've learned that expertise isn't built overnight. Hiring the right people isn't just about capability—it's about finding those whose values mirror our own, who understand that excellence without alignment falls short. She paused, tapping a finger lightly against the table. "And let's not forget the reality of the hiring landscape. It's not just about finding someone who meets our standards—it's about timing. The right candidate must be available when we need them, willing to grow within our structure, and, frankly, within the salary range we've established. Otherwise, we're back to square one, stretching ourselves too thin while we search for the 'perfect fit' who may not exist on our timeline."

Without a word, James tapped back into his iPad, logging key points with practiced precision. "Internal expansion—like what we did with the SSRP team—has clear advantages. We maintain full control, ensuring alignment with our values and client-first philosophy. The SSRP pilot demonstrated the power of organic growth when we nurture talent from within. But the downside is capacity. Finding the right people isn't just about skill; they need to fit our culture, and the hiring process itself is time-intensive. Even when we find someone who checks all the boxes, onboarding and training take months, sometimes longer. And we need to be mindful of salary expectations within our budget and timeline."

Nicole moved to the next slide. "Now, external partnerships—those come with a different set of advantages. They give us flexibility, allowing us to scale services up or down as needed. But trust would be a hurdle. We'd need partners who not only provide expertise but also match the level of credibility and client relationships we've built. If we don't get that right, it could weaken everything we've worked to establish."

James returned to his iPad, reading his notes with his usual measured focus. "External expansion looks less expensive on the surface," he said without looking up, "especially if we avoid hiring full-time right away. But we would have to be careful not to become dependent on someone who sees their value rise and starts demanding more than we're comfortable paying. That kind of leverage can turn quickly."

He paused, tapping the screen once to emphasize the point. "Scalability is great. But only if it doesn't come at the cost of control."

He set the iPad down and leaned back slightly. "So that's the real question: Do we invest in long-term internal growth, knowing it takes more time and resources? Or do we prioritize flexibility by bringing in external specialists who can help us scale faster, but at the risk of losing control over the client experience? Trust is the biggest hurdle. We need partners who operate with the same client-first commitment that defines us. That kind of alignment isn't automatic—it's built over time, and any misstep could shake the client's confidence and solid reputation that we've spent years establishing. So, we have two paths. One gives us control but demands a significant investment of time and resources. The other offers agility but requires an equally careful vetting process to ensure we don't compromise on trust. The question is—where do we gain the most without losing what makes us, us?"

Nicole remained silent for a moment; the usual quick-fire response held back as she weighed the options carefully. Her gaze flickered between James and the slides she had prepared, the pause itself speaking to the complexity of the decision. "Both approaches have merit, but the real question is: which gives us the agility to evolve with client needs? Health and wealth planning are shifting faster than ever. If we expand internally but miscalculate, we could end up with specialists who don't fit, or worse, resources tied up in the wrong areas. But if we lean too heavily on external partnerships, we risk diluting the client experience. We've built trust by being hands-on, by guiding them through every step. We can't afford to lose that."

The room fell silent for a moment, the potential consequence of the decision settling over them. This wasn't just about growth—it was about defining the future of their firm.

Finally, Nicole broke the silence. "We map it out in phases," she said, her tone decisive. "A hybrid approach. Phase one: We refine our internal growth model. The SSRP was successful, but it required hands-on involvement from both of us. This time, we need to create a framework where specialized expertise develops organically, without us steering every detail." After a moment, Nicole adds, "Which means hiring strategically, setting up structured mentorships, paying for certifications and training, and staying close enough to the program to ensure any new specialists align with our client-first philosophy from day one."

James glanced up from his note-taking, then added, "And maybe we don't need to look outside right away. There could be people on our team already—people we've overlooked—who have the potential to grow into these roles with the right support."

Nicole's eyes sparkled with approval, her smile warm and genuine. "That's exactly the kind of thinking we need," she said, clearly energized. "Before we search the market, let's inventory our own bench. What if the talent's already here and just needs a path forward?"

She paused, letting the idea take root before continuing. "At the same time, we lay the groundwork for external partnerships in areas where we aren't ready for full-time hires. That gives us flexibility to expand without rushing into commitments that could strain resources."

James looked up from his iPad, his expression serious. "That gives us an opportunity to evaluate both models. We can measure client satisfaction, service efficiency, and the impact on growth. If something isn't working, we pivot."

"Exactly," Nicole replied, her confidence growing. "And we need metrics—clear ones. Gut instincts got us here, but they won't take us further. Client feedback, operational efficiency, financial outcomes—we track everything."

For the next hour, they worked methodically, outlining the plan with precision. Immediate actions, timelines, and responsibilities came into focus. Nicole took the lead in identifying and vetting potential partners, developing a rigorous selection process to ensure alignment with the firm's core values, and incorporating subject matter that would lead to improved retirement planning. James assumed responsibility for recruiting in-house talent, ensuring they uncovered, if available, the expertise needed to meet the firm's evolving demands.

"We also need a communication strategy for our clients," Nicole added. "They need to see how these changes benefit them directly. Whether it's internal specialists or external partnerships, transparency will be critical to maintaining their trust."

By the time they finished, the plan was no longer just a collection of ideas—it was a clear, actionable strategy. Each phase had measurable outcomes, each responsibility was defined, and the flexibility to adapt was built in. This wasn't just a vision anymore. It was a deliberate and unshakable drive forward.

What came next was the true test—not more thinking, but more doing.

With clarity in hand, James and Nicole turned their attention to building a blueprint—a playbook—that could guide execution across the firm. The strategy had to develop beyond their iPads, computers, and conversations—it needed to scale, empower others, and hold up under pressure.

CHAPTER 13

From Strategy to Implementation:

A Step-by-Step Growth Strategy Playbook

With their strategic foundation in place, James and Nicole were ready to move beyond insight and into execution. They had defined their values, identified their growth channels, and started cultivating a team culture ready for change. But scaling a firm into a retirement leadership brand meant more than ambition—it required precision.

What follows is their **Step-by-Step Growth Strategy Playbook**—a framework grounded in Covey's principles, enriched by insights from pilot programs, and sharpened by the operational innovations that Nicole championed. It was Nicole's forward-thinking mindset that led the firm to embrace AI, not as a replacement for human expertise, but as a catalyst for deeper personalization, greater efficiency, and smarter decision-making. Under her guidance, the firm began integrating AI-powered tools to analyze data patterns, enhance outreach, and automate routine tasks, allowing their team to stay focused on what mattered most: the client relationship.

This playbook outlines how they built capacity through internal development and external collaboration, how they protected their brand while expanding their service offerings, and how they integrated business succession, family legacy, healthcare, and contingency planning into a unified retirement strategy.

Each step is designed to help their firm—and any firm—grow intentionally, with purpose, people, and progress working in harmony.

What began as an awakening had evolved into a structured, two-path growth strategy: one route focused on organic development—deepening capabilities from within—and the other on external expansion, building a carefully curated ecosystem of partners and specialists. What follows is the operational heart of their transformation—a detailed playbook to guide not only their firm, but any advisory practice seeking to lead with purpose in a world where retirement is no longer just about wealth, but about well-being.

◆◆◆

Implementing Option A: Organic Growth

To grow internally, they identified key steps and adopted a deliberate approach to recruiting the talent required for their Business Growth Plan.

Step 1: Identify Core Needs and Gaps

They began with an internal audit, analyzing client feedback and projecting future demands. Healthcare costs, extended retirements, and complex wealth management needs intersect in ways their current expertise couldn't fully address. The solution? Hiring specialists in Medicare, short-term, extended, and long-term care, work interruptions, insurance, and non-insurance options to bridge the gaps and enhance client outcomes.

Step 2: Create a Strategic Recruitment Plan

Nicole and James crafted a profile of their ideal candidates: seeking individuals who qualified as skilled professionals and who would likely be deeply attuned to the firm's client-first values. Cultural alignment was non-negotiable. Their new hires had to embody collaboration, expertise in their specialty, credibility, and empathy, ensuring the firm's environment remained supportive and client-centric.

Step 3: Budget for Success

Armed with financial models, James calculated the costs—salaries, benefits, and onboarding—and weighed them against projected returns. Beyond the numbers, they anticipated potential challenges. How would new team members integrate into existing workflows? Could the firm's culture thrive amid this expansion? Processes for cultural integration and early problem resolution were to be baked into the recruitment strategy. Acknowledging that they were building expertise from scratch in areas like Medicare planning and long-term care, Nicole and James developed an alternative approach to ensure smooth onboarding and alignment with the firm's values:

- **Cultural Immersion Sessions**: New hires would participate in intensive workshops led by Nicole or James, focusing on the firm's mission, core values, and client-first ethos. These sessions would include case studies from the firm's history, illustrating the nuanced approach to integrating lifespan, health span, and wealth span in retirement planning.
- **Structured Cross-Training**: While these areas were new to the firm, Nicole and James recognized the importance of interdisciplinary collaboration. New specialists would work closely with existing team members in areas like investment management, retirement planning, and legacy planning, ensuring a holistic understanding of how their expertise fits into the larger picture.

- **Open-Forum Integration Meetings**: Nicole would host monthly meetings during the first six months, inviting new hires to discuss their experiences, suggest improvements, and address any challenges they encountered. These forums would encourage transparency and foster a sense of inclusion, helping to identify and resolve potential conflicts early.
- **Continuous Professional Development**: To foster a sense of community among new hires, the firm would sponsor small-group attendance at industry conferences, workshops, and certifications. This shared growth experience would help establish camaraderie while sharpening skills. By focusing on structured learning and fostering collaboration from day one, James and Nicole aimed to seamlessly weave new talent into the fabric of their firm, ensuring that both client expectations and internal culture remained uncompromised.

Step 4: Evaluate and Course-Correct

Hiring wasn't a one-and-done solution—it was the beginning of an ongoing process. Some roles might be filled externally, but others could come from within. James and Nicole recognized the untapped potential among their current staff and committed to creating clear pathways for internal promotion. Anyone stepping into a new role—whether hired or promoted—would undergo a structured trial period, with defined benchmarks around client engagement, communication skills, and technical capability.

They also planned to occasionally sit in on client meetings or review interactions, ensuring that every team member reflected the firm's client-first values and possessed the expertise. Regular performance reviews and feedback loops would track progress, client satisfaction, and service outcomes to ensure ongoing improvement. If a team member wasn't enhancing the client experience or aligning with the firm's direction, they'd address it promptly. Flexibility, accountability, and support would guide every decision in this phase of growth.

Implementing Option B: External Partnerships

To expand externally, they explored building a network of trusted specialists to complement the firm's services.

Step 1: Identify Strategic Partners

Nicole and James knew that external partnerships couldn't be left to chance. To build a reliable bench of subject-matter experts, they created a targeted strategy for identifying professionals who aligned with the firm's mission. They began compiling a list of standout voices in retirement tax planning, Social Security, Medicare, and caregiving—key areas where specialized expertise could elevate the client experience.

They attended conferences and webinars, not just to learn, but to observe how experts presented, communicated, and engaged with audiences. They read articles and thought and innovation pieces from industry leaders, paying close attention to tone and alignment with their client-first values. Social media also became a powerful tool—LinkedIn, industry groups, and professional forums helped them uncover rising voices and established professionals whose philosophies matched their own.

Their criteria were clear: these professionals needed to be more than just technically competent. They had to demonstrate empathy, clarity, and the ability to translate complex topics into meaningful guidance for clients.

This growing roster of vetted specialists became more than a referral list—it was a strategic asset. Each expert represented an extension of the firm's promise to provide not just financial advice, but comprehensive, human-centered planning.

Step 2: Develop a Win-Win Collaboration Model

Collaboration models—ranging from simple referral agreements to more structured profit-sharing arrangements—were explored to incentivize mutual success and drive shared growth. These models enabled James and Nicole to establish a network of trusted specialists who were invested not only in their own outcomes but also in the shared success of the client relationship.

For some professionals, a referral relationship was sufficient, built on trust, communication, and mutual respect. For others, especially those offering recurring value or ongoing support, profit-sharing became an attractive option. These agreements were carefully structured to ensure alignment of interests without compromising transparency or independence.

This multi-tiered approach enabled the firm to dramatically expand its service offerings—tax planning, Medicare navigation, elder law, caregiving strategy—without incurring the fixed overhead of full-time hires. Instead of building everything in-house, they created a responsive, modular team that could be scaled up or down as needed. It maintained flexibility, preserved capital, and most importantly, delivered value to clients without sacrificing quality.

By treating these collaborations as business accelerators—not just extensions of client service—James and Nicole turned external partnerships into a powerful growth lever for the firm.

Step 3: Formalize and Build Trust

Recognizing the importance of transparency, they engaged legal counsel to draft comprehensive agreements. These contracts outlined roles, responsibilities, and financial terms while safeguarding client trust and avoiding conflicts of interest.

Step 4: Communicate the Value Proposition

Growth wasn't just about adding services—it was about making sure clients understood the value of those additions. Drawing on the insights gained from their pilot projects, James and Nicole developed a clear communication strategy designed to position their network of experts as a natural extension of the firm's core offering.

This was more than a tactical update—it was a branding evolution. They aligned their messaging across every touchpoint, including the website, client meetings, email newsletters, and onboarding materials. The goal was to reinforce that these specialists weren't outsiders—they were carefully vetted partners, brought in to serve the same mission: helping clients retire with clarity, confidence, and dignity.

They trained their advisors to discuss these partnerships not as extras, but as integral parts of a comprehensive planning experience. Healthcare, wealthcare, Longevity Literacy, Social Security, tax strategy, caregiving—these weren't side topics anymore. They were pillars of a modern, holistic financial plan.

By framing their evolution as a firm-wide commitment to leadership in retirement readiness, James and Nicole ensured their clients didn't just see more services—they saw a firm that had grown alongside them, ready to guide the next chapter.

Step 5: Rebrand to Reflect Retirement Leadership

The firm had officially shifted from traditional wealth management to trusted retirement leadership. To reflect that evolution, James and Nicole recognized the need for a strategic rebranding initiative. This wasn't just about updating visuals; it was about clearly communicating their broader role in clients' lives.

They began by revisiting the firm's messaging. The website was redesigned to emphasize holistic retirement planning, integrating the roles of longevity, wealth, and health. Service pages were rewritten to highlight outcomes and real-life impact, not just offerings. Everything pointed back to a singular message: *Retirement isn't just a number. It's a journey—and we're here to help you lead it, not just survive it.*

The visual identity evolved too—colors and imagery shifted from purely financial tones to ones representing vitality, longevity, and family well-being. A refined tagline brought the message home:

"Plan with Purpose. Retire with Confidence."

Internally, team training reinforced the rebrand. Everyone—from client service staff to senior advisors—was equipped to speak the new language of retirement leadership. Every touchpoint became an opportunity to deliver clarity, empathy, and value.

For James and Nicole, the rebrand wasn't cosmetic. It was cultural. It affirmed the firm's identity as more than a financial services provider—it was a planning partner for the long game of life.

Step 6: Continuously Monitor and Optimize

Partnerships, they knew, weren't "set it and forget it" arrangements. Like any relationship rooted in trust, they required intentional nurturing and consistent oversight. To ensure these alliances remained aligned with the firm's standards and evolved with client needs, James and Nicole designed a robust framework to manage external collaborators effectively:

- **Flexible Agreements:** Each partnership was built on adaptable contracts that allowed for regular review and recalibration. Rather than locking themselves into long-term commitments, they favored agreements that could evolve alongside shifting generational client needs and performance results. This flexibility ensured the firm could scale wisely, without sacrificing control.
- **Structured Evaluations:** Performance wasn't judged by gut instinct alone. Nicole and James implemented regular assessments using specific metrics, including client satisfaction scores, clarity of communication, turnaround times, and the expert's adherence to the firm's values in client interactions. These evaluations were logged and reviewed on a quarterly basis.

- **Trial Phases:** Every new partnership begins with a trial period. This allowed both parties to assess fit without pressure. During this time, the expert would be introduced selectively to clients, while James or Nicole observed initial meetings and gathered feedback. It was a deliberate filter—a proving ground before formal inclusion on the firm's advisory roster.
- **Client Feedback Loops:** Most importantly, they made it easy for clients to share their impressions. Whether through informal follow-up conversations or brief satisfaction surveys, James and Nicole utilized client input to inform their decision-making. If a specialist didn't uphold the firm's service standards, the partnership was swiftly re-evaluated.

Together, these measures protected the firm's core identity while enabling growth through collaboration. Each new expert wasn't just an outside resource—they were carefully chosen, well-managed allies in the client journey.

- **Reciprocal Referral Flow:** But what surprised them most—and proved to be a game-changer—was the opportunity for reciprocal growth. The same specialists they had introduced to clients began referring individuals back to them. These were clients looking for more than a one-dimensional advisor; they were ready for the bigger picture. By positioning the firm as a leader in retirement planning—not just investment strategy—James and Nicole became the trusted next step for clients introduced by elder law attorneys, CPAs, Medicare advisors, and care consultants. The result was a steady pipeline of aligned, high-quality prospects—clients who already understood and appreciated the value of holistic planning.

Together, these strategies transformed their partnerships from simple service enhancements into a true engine for growth—economically, operationally, and reputationally. Each collaborator wasn't just an external resource; they were a business ally, a value amplifier, and a key to long-term scalability.

◆◆◆

Steering Toward Growth

James and Nicole were in their usual conference room spot, now more of a command center than a meeting space. The air between them carried the quiet satisfaction of follow-through. Their strategy wasn't just drafted; it was alive. A working plan. A blueprint with teeth.

As they gathered their things, James glanced at the clock. For the first time in a while, he didn't feel behind. Time wasn't chasing them—they were steering it.

Nicole shot him a playful glance, her voice light but meaningful. "We've got this. But if I see even one lonely spreadsheet collecting dust—or worse, sense you slipping back into your number cave—I'll treat you like a client who forgot their login."

James laughed, hand over heart in mock pledge. "Spreadsheets in motion. Promise."

With that, they stepped out of the room, not just carrying plans but carrying momentum. They were no longer responding to a shifting landscape—they were reshaping it. Retirement planning wasn't just about accumulation anymore. It was about dignity, flexibility, and legacy. And now, with a plan in hand, it was time to test the strategy in action.

CHAPTER 14

Camera, Places and... Action!

The Longevity Literacy Gathering

The firm's main conference room buzzed—not with nerves, but with purpose. Tonight marked the launch of their first Longevity Literacy Gathering, a new series designed to educate and elevate. This wasn't a marketing event. It was a mindset shift—an intentional gathering centered around genuine questions, genuine anxieties, and practical solutions.

More than 10,000 Baby Boomers were turning 65 every day, and Nicole had insisted they start strong: by confronting the elephant in the retirement room—**the true cost of aging.** Not just financially, but emotionally, physically, and logistically. It was time to talk about extended care. Not in the abstract, but in specifics. And not just from them, but from a trusted voice from their roster of external experts.

Tonight, they had invited an extended care specialist to lead the session, an expert well-versed in the realities of Medicare limitations, insurance, and non-insurance options, as well as caregiving strategies. It was the first real application of their external expansion strategy—and a test of how clients would respond to being served in a more expansive, integrated way.

By first exposing the risks of inaction, they could create urgency—an undeniable catalyst—before guiding participants toward a proactive roadmap for securing their future. James considered the approach carefully and agreed: before discussing *how* to plan for retirement, clients needed to understand *why* planning couldn't wait.

James stood at the podium, aligning his notes with steady precision, while Nicole moved through the room, greeting clients with her signature warmth and wit. The space was filled with a mix of familiar faces and curious newcomers, all drawn by the promise of something beyond the usual financial seminar—something deeper, more essential.

For months, James and Nicole had poured their energy into redefining the firm's approach. Retirement planning had evolved beyond spreadsheets and portfolio reviews; their clients sought guidance on the complex intersections of wealth, health, and longevity. These Longevity Literacy Gatherings would become more than educational sessions—they were the bridge between uncertainty and preparedness. Clients would no longer come just for financial updates; they would come seeking clarity on everything from optimizing income streams to navigating Medicare and crafting sustainable aging-in-place strategies.

As clients settled into their seats, a gentle undercurrent of neo-classical ambient music filled the room—soft, contemplative compositions by Max Richter, Ólafur Arnalds, and Ludovico Einaudi. The seamless blend of modern and classical elements created an atmosphere of quiet focus, reinforcing the professional yet inviting tone James and Nicole had carefully cultivated for the gathering. The music wasn't intrusive; it was a subtle cue, setting the stage for deep reflection and meaningful discussion.

Nicole adjusted the lighting, dimming the fluorescents just slightly to create a more intimate tone. Clients trickled in—some with notebooks, others with skeptical glances—but all carrying the weight of questions they hadn't yet asked aloud. James greeted familiar faces with his usual steadiness, but even he felt the difference. This wasn't a portfolio review or tax strategy session. This was bigger.

Dan, the long-term care specialist they had brought in, stood confidently near the front. He wasn't flashy, but he was grounded, seasoned by hundreds of conversations with families blindsided by the harsh realities of aging. Nicole gave him a quick nod from across the room, signaling it was time.

James stepped forward, his voice steady, his tone practiced but not rehearsed. "Welcome, everyone. It's great to see so many familiar faces—and a few new ones, too. Today, we're diving into one of the least predictable aspects of retirement: healthcare costs, specifically extended and long-term care costs."

Nicole, standing to his right, injected her signature levity. "And let's be honest—who hasn't wished for a crystal ball lately? Unfortunately, Amazon's fresh out, so instead, we're relying on something better: solid planning and expert advice. "Luckily, we've brought in an expert to help us tackle this at tonight's Longevity Literacy Gathering, Dan M."

Dan stepped forward. He shifted his stance, grounding himself with deliberate poise, the depth of decades of insight evident in his demeanor. "Thank you for inviting me. I'd like to start with a story that perfectly illustrates why preparation matters. In 1923, a man named Garrett Morgan was driving through Cleveland when he witnessed a terrible car accident at an intersection. There were no traffic signals at the time—just a chaotic mix of drivers, horses, and pedestrians all navigating the roads without structure or guidance. That moment sparked an idea, and Morgan went on to invent the modern three-position traffic signal—an innovation that has saved countless lives ever since.

The lesson? Systems and planning prevent chaos. Retirement and longevity planning work similarly. Without a clear roadmap, unexpected events—an illness, a caregiving crisis, a financial downturn—can derail not just your retirement but your relationships, your health, and your legacy. Tonight, we'll explore how to put the right safeguards in place, ensuring that your future isn't left to chance but guided by intention."

The audience responded with knowing smiles and murmurs of appreciation, the story's unexpected lesson settling in.

"Morgan didn't rely on luck to help people safely cross the street—he created a system, a plan that provided order and security. In the same way, hoping for the best in extended or long-term care planning isn't a strategy—it's a risk. Without a clear plan, you're not just rolling the dice on your own future, but on the well-being of your family as well. Retirement healthcare costs aren't just a footnote—they're a blind spot."

The room stilled.

"And as people live longer than ever—into their 90s, and increasingly past 100—the need for extended care is rising fast," Dan began, his voice composed but direct. "But most Americans are still planning as if they won't need it."

He let that sink in before continuing.

"The U.S. Census Bureau projects that the number of centenarians—people living past 100—will quadruple by 2054. That's not a projection to ignore. Living longer doesn't automatically mean living healthier. It means more years where care may be needed—and more opportunities for costs to quietly accumulate."

A few heads nodded. Others leaned in, listening more closely.

"And yet," Dan said, clicking to the next slide, "a 2025 study from the Nationwide Retirement Institute shows that 41% of Americans believe they won't live long enough to need long-term care. That assumption isn't just overly optimistic—it's dangerous."

Nicole glanced toward James. He was watching the room, seeing what they'd both suspected: clients were taking this in not with fear, but with focus.

Dan's voice steadied. "The same study found that nearly 70% of Americans turning 65 this year *will* need some form of long-term care. That's the reality. And if we don't plan for it, that gap between what people expect and what actually happens?- that gap can quietly dismantle even the most well-built retirement plan."

He paused, letting the weight of those words settle.

"And it gets more concerning," he continued. "One of the biggest misconceptions I hear—almost daily—is this idea that Medicare will cover long-term care. It won't."

Dan stepped forward slightly, scanning the room. "Fifty-eight percent of Americans still believe that Medicare will pay for long-term care costs. However, Medicare was never designed to cover the kind of help aging people often need—help with activities such as bathing, dressing, eating, or managing medications on a daily basis. That's not just a misunderstanding—it's a liability."

He clicked again, displaying a side-by-side chart that shows what Medicare *covers* and *what it does not.*

"Before we talk about solutions, we must be clear-eyed about the problem. We are living longer. We are living with more chronic conditions. And most people are either unprepared or misinformed."

The room had gone still.

Nicole and James exchanged a knowing look.

This is why we built the plan.

Dan reached for his water as Nicole gave the room a moment to absorb his words, then glanced toward Dan with a smile that was both genuine and just a touch mischievous.

"Alright," she said, shifting her weight and glancing around. "Let's be honest—talking about extended care and long-term care? Extended care, aging, what Medicare won't cover… not exactly what you were hoping for after dinner, right?" The upside is that it's basically the fastest way to clear the room at a cocktail party. Which is a great tactic if you ever want the hors d'oeuvres to yourself."

Laughter broke the tension, and a few people nodded knowingly.

"But that's exactly why we're offering the Longevity Literacy Gathering Series," she continued, tone softening. "These aren't easy conversations—but they are necessary. Not to scare you, but to prepare you. Because let's be honest: none of us wants to be caught off guard, especially not when it comes to our health or our money."

She paused, then let a little edge back into her voice. "And yes, I know you've got questions—Medicare Advantage, supplemental insurance, drug plans, donut holes… and don't even get me started on enrollment deadlines. That's why we're bringing in a Medicare specialist for one of our upcoming Longevity Literacy Gatherings."

"But tonight? We're talking about *the* cost. The one that doesn't hit all at once, but sneaks in slowly and refuses to leave. Extended care. The kind that could unravel your retirement plan if it's not addressed. This is the stuff people avoid talking about until it's right at their doorstep. But you're here. And that means you're not waiting until crisis mode."

She turned toward Dan, motioning him forward. "So, I'm handing it back to Dan. He's got the real numbers, the real risks, and yes—the real options. Let's dig in."

Dan stepped up, smiling as Nicole moved to the side.

"No pressure, right?" he quipped.

Nicole grinned. "Just make it better than my cocktail party story.

The room grew quiet as he continued, his tone deliberate. "Let's consider the rising costs of long-term care. From in-home assistance to nursing homes, the financial burden can escalate rapidly, especially over several years. These expenses aren't just disruptive—they can jeopardize even the most carefully constructed financial plans if they aren't accounted for ahead of time."

Dan paused again, allowing the audience to absorb his message. "The objective here isn't to scare you; it's to educate and prepare you. Whether through traditional long-term care insurance, hybrid policies, Health Savings Accounts, or other strategies, addressing these costs before they arise ensures your financial security and preserves the legacy you've worked so hard to build."

He gestured toward the presentation screen, which displayed projections for escalating extended and long-term care costs and workforce shortages. "It's not just about affording these services today—it's about understanding how shortages in healthcare professionals and rising wages are pushing costs higher every year. And we're still in the midst of the Baby Boomer generation aging into a stage of life where these services and supports are increasingly critical. This unprecedented demand is creating a ripple effect, driving costs up and placing more strain on already stretched resources."

He paused and then continued. "This doesn't just affect retirees. Whether you're caring for aging parents, assisting a loved one, or planning for your own future, these expenses can undermine your financial goals and create stress that careens through every aspect of your life. Many of us envision retirement as the reward for years of hard work—a time to relax and savor life. But without a comprehensive plan for extended and long-term care, those golden years can quickly shift from a season of peace to one overshadowed by financial strain and emotional stress."

Nicole stepped forward, breaking the tension with her signature wit. "Let's understand it for what it is—it's not Monopoly money. If you don't plan ahead, it's game over, and nobody likes flipping the board."

The humor broke the heavy atmosphere and drew a few smiles or nods. James followed seamlessly, his tone reflective and firm, "Nicole's right—these costs are far from trivial. These unplanned expenses can throw your entire financial plan into chaos. Legacy goals, tax strategies, and even the ability to continue growing your investments can be compromised. The time to act is now, before these challenges become crises."

Nicole shifted her attention from James back to the audience, her hand sweeping over the audience with quiet command. "That's precisely why we've gathered tonight—to turn understanding into action, to prepare for the future with clarity instead of chance. Whether it's understanding caregiver services, identifying tax-efficient strategies, or simply knowing where to turn for support, planning today makes all the difference tomorrow."

She turned toward Dan with a warm smile, her tone infused with charm. "Your insights have been nothing short of illuminating—thank you for sparking the kind of conversations that truly matter," she said, her words breaking the thoughtful silence that lingered in the room. Then, addressing the group, she added with a lighter tone, "Before we dive into questions, we've set up refreshments in the lounge. Take a moment to grab some coffee or tea, relax, and let everything sink in. We'll reconvene shortly."

As clients mingled, their conversations took on a reflective tone. By the coffee station, a small group lingered, exchanging thoughts sparked by the presentation. "I thought I could self-insure," one woman admitted, her voice tinged with uncertainty, "but now I'm not so sure. Risking my legacy, even just a part of what I want my grandchildren to inherit, feels... reckless."

Another attendee nodded in agreement. "It's a relief to know we're not expected to figure this out alone. The options are way more numerous than I ever imagined. Tonight gave me hope—there's a path forward."

Across the room, a man leaned toward his wife, his tone quieter but no less resolute. "I've avoided thinking about aging," he murmured, "but this is a wake-up call. We need to act."

Holding their forgotten coffee, a couple stood in quiet conversation, their expressions marked by equal parts concern and resolve. The husband turned toward his wife, his voice low but steady. "I have no idea what the plan is for my father, and he's really starting to show his age. With our two sons in high school—and all the chaos that brings—moving him in with us just isn't realistic."

His wife nodded; her brows knitted in thought. "We need to figure out our options—and his—before we're backed into a corner. The last thing any of us needs is to be forced into a situation filled with tension, conflict, and unplanned expenses."

The two fell silent for a moment, their worry hanging between them like an unspoken question. They weren't alone in their predicament, but for now, it felt as if the weight of planning had landed squarely on their shoulders.

When the group reconvened for the Q&A, the atmosphere had shifted. The earlier quiet contemplation had given way to lively engagement. Clients stood up to ask questions, others leaned forward, their questions sharp and deliberate—not just theoretical, but personal. They weren't just absorbing information anymore; they were applying it, connecting it to their own lives.

James, Nicole, with Dan's help, fielded each inquiry with precision, striking a balance between expertise and empathy. Some questions had clear, straightforward answers. Others unraveled into deeper discussions, underscoring the complexity of planning for longevity, healthcare, and financial stability.

Nicole, ever the bridge between information and action, handled the tougher questions with her signature mix of candor and warmth. "That's an excellent point," she acknowledged to one particularly nuanced query. "And exactly why these gatherings aren't meant to be one-and-done events. Tonight isn't just about walking away with answers—it's about walking away with better questions. The kind that leads to real, intentional planning."

A murmur of agreement rippled through the group. Couples exchanged glances, some already mentally drafting the questions they'd take home, the conversations they'd finally start.

She glanced around the room, reading the energy, letting unspoken thoughts fill the space. "Real change happens when you take what clicked for you tonight and do something with it—when you sit down, have the tough conversations, and make a plan that works for you and your family—preferably before life smacks you upside the head. What risks need to be addressed? What gaps need to be filled? What conversations have been avoided for too long?

She stepped forward slightly, voice warm but purposeful. "This gathering is the spark. But the real change? That starts when you turn that spark into action."

She pointed gently toward a small table near the exit. "Before you leave, we invite you to stop by and schedule a follow-up appointment with one of our team members—we're here to help. Or, call us after you have a chance to think through what would be helpful in your situation. If tonight made you think, let's turn that into a plan you can count on."

James joined Suzanne at the front of the room, his expression reflecting a quiet sense of pride and gratitude. "Thank you all for coming tonight," he began, scanning the room. "Some of you brought your spouses. Some brought their parents. A few of you are here for the first time, just beginning to think about these questions. Wherever you are on this journey, we're honored you chose to spend your time with us."

He paused, his tone steady and sincere. "These conversations aren't always easy, but they're important. And tonight, we started one together. Let's not let it end here. Let's keep it going—in our offices, around your kitchen tables, and in the plans we build together."

He offered a relaxed smile. "Our team is here for you. We're not just planning for retirement—we're helping you build a future that feels secure, informed, and fully your own."

As a few guests began to gather near the signup sheets, James stepped back, letting the room move around him. Watching the interactions unfold—clients exchanging thoughts, adult children thanking staff, even newcomers lingering to ask one more question—he felt a flicker of something deeper than professional satisfaction.

It was a realization—one he hadn't fully grasped until now.

This wasn't just about strategy. It wasn't even just about planning.

It was about trust. It was about showing up for people before life forced their hand. And for the first time in a long time, James didn't feel like a financial advisor navigating risk. He felt like a partner in something more meaningful. And in that moment, he knew this was the work worth doing.

From Awareness to Action

The next morning, James and Nicole met for coffee in the conference room—this time without charts or client files, just two mugs and the quiet satisfaction of a night that had gone exactly as planned.

James leaned back in his chair, his expression thoughtful. "Last night felt different," he said. "Not just because of the turnout, but the tone. The way people engaged."

Nicole nodded, still riding the energy of the evening. "We opened a door that's been locked for too long. Extended care isn't a product—it's a conversation. It wasn't about products or checklists. It was about gathering information and facts that would help them confront what most people avoid—how aging really unfolds, and what it demands from a family. Extended care touches on identity, legacy, and relationships, not just finances."

James looked at her, a tiny flicker of excitement surfacing. "So, we build on that trust. That was a specialty gathering. The next one—it's the framework. A roadmap session."

Nicole smiled. "Exactly. We take what we learned and offer a path forward—bigger, broader. A session designed to help them connect the dots from longevity to lifestyle, from uncertainty to action. This one's not just about planning for one risk—it's about preparing for their personal whole journey."

James nodded, already envisioning the next event. "Not a seminar. A strategy session. Something they can walk away from with confidence."

Nicole arched an eyebrow. "You're thinking roadmap?"

James smiled. "Exactly. We saw that extended care was a planning spark, and that's great. But what about using that same knowledge format and making the next Longevity Literacy Gathering about structure, providing clients with a framework they can build around? Planning not just for health and longevity, but for transitions, priorities, finances, and futures."

Nicole nodded, the next phase already taking shape in his mind. "So, we move from spotlight to strategy. I like it."

And with that, the next Gathering was set in motion—not just a continuation, but an expansion. One that would help clients move from isolated concerns to an integrated vision of their retirement future.

CHAPTER 15

The Longevity Literacy Gathering

The Longevity Roadmap

Two weeks later, the shift in the room was unmistakable—not in volume, but in tone. While a few familiar faces had returned from the earlier Extended Care Gathering, most of tonight's attendees were new, drawn in by more than word of mouth. This time, they were answering a different call—one sparked by the firm's bold rebranding effort.

Gone were the traditional taglines about market performance and asset growth. In their place stood a new identity: **"Plan with Purpose. Retire with Confidence"**—a brand rooted in trust, empathy, and longevity literacy. The messaging was simple but powerful: *Retirement isn't just a number. It's a journey—and we're here to help you lead it, not just survive it.*

This wasn't a crowd looking for another generic retirement seminar. These were individuals and families who understood, or at least suspected, the stakes and wanted a plan they could trust.

Nicole, with her trademark mix of humor and warmth, stepped up to welcome them.

"Welcome to our Longevity Literacy Gathering. If you're here, it means one thing—you're ready to stop hoping things work out and start designing a plan that tilts the odds in your favor!" She grinned. "And if a few of you are back for another round of my stand-up routine, don't worry—I take requests."

A few chuckles rippled through the crowd, creating a sense of ease.

James joined Nicole at the front of the room, his usual calm presence now underscored by a quiet urgency. This wasn't just about sharing insights—it was about translating those insights into strategy.

"If you missed our last session, we focused on extended care—what happens when aging gets complicated. But tonight's session is broader. This is about building your full longevity roadmap—from healthcare to legacy, from lifestyle to protection strategies. It's not just what could go wrong—it's how to build a plan that helps everything go right."

He let that settle before continuing.

"Think of this roadmap as a living document. A compass that guides not just your money, but your decisions—what to prepare for, what to protect, and what to prioritize. Knowledge is only powerful if you use it. So, this isn't just about gaining knowledge anymore—it's about applying it. And you're not navigating it alone."

Nicole gestured to the screen, where key steps were displayed. The first: *Identify Your Priorities.*

"This is where it begins—what matters most to *you.* Independence? Security? Flexibility? Supporting family? That's what your roadmap will be built around. So, let's get started."

"We begin by focusing on what matters most to you—whether it's ensuring loved ones are cared for, preserving your independence, protecting your assets and income, or your legacy. Every journey is unique, and your roadmap will reflect those personal priorities."

James continued seamlessly. "From there, we integrate expertise. Whether it's an in-house specialist or a member of our extended network, these trusted advisors bring the knowledge needed to craft actionable strategies. Their input ensures your roadmap is grounded in your realities."

Nicole rounded out the introduction with a tone that was reassuring. "The Longevity Literacy Gatherings are more than just sessions—they're your connection to a team of experts who will guide you through every phase. This collaboration is how we turn ideas into action. And it starts tonight."

James, his tone measured and practical, continued, "From there, we address the 'how.' This includes assessing your current financial strategies, incorporating tax-efficient care planning, and building contingencies for unforeseen longevity expenses, such as a change in housing or an unexpected dependency. The goal is to create a plan that not only sustains you but adapts to life's changes."

Nicole added a note of reassurance. "The beauty of this process is that you're not doing it alone. Our team is available to guide you every step of the way, ensuring that your roadmap isn't just theoretical—it's actionable and tailored to your unique needs."

She continued, "This process isn't about tackling everything at once. It's about taking deliberate, meaningful steps toward securing your future. The first step is simple yet profound: evaluate your needs."

James stepped forward as the lights dimmed slightly, the screen behind him casting a soft glow across the room. "Tonight isn't about having all the answers," he began, his tone measured and inviting. "It's about starting the right conversations—the ones that shape the roadmap for your future."

He gestured toward the slide behind him: *Your Longevity Roadmap – Let's Build It Together.*

"This working session is your opportunity to begin. We'll walk you through three key steps designed to help you clarify your longevity priorities—whether that's your finances, health, family, or lifestyle—and set the stage for a more personalized plan. Our role is to help you take what matters most and turn it into action."

As James spoke, Nicole and their team moved through the room, placing worksheets and checklists on each table. "Our team is here to support you,"

Nicole added, addressing the group with a warm smile. "Ask questions, bounce around ideas, or just reflect quietly if that's more your style. But start. Because from here, we can help you find the specialists, tools, and strategies that match your unique situation."

With that, participants leaned in, pens and tablets in hand. Around the room, a quiet sense of purpose settled in—not urgency, but thoughtful intent. This wasn't just another seminar. It was the groundwork for a new kind of partnership—one where each attendee would begin shaping their future with clarity, support, and the right resources.

James advanced the slide, revealing three core categories for building their personal roadmap: Health & Longevity, Wealth & Legacy, and Family & Lifestyle. As participants began to explore these areas, the room shifted into quiet activity—questions emerged, ideas formed, and plans started to take root.

1. Evaluate Your Longevity Needs:

Longevity planning isn't just about adding years to your life—it's about making those years meaningful. Tonight's session may have sparked thoughts across several areas. Now it's time to organize them.

Reflect Across Life Domains: As you think back on tonight's discussion, ask yourself:

- Health: Am I prepared for the healthcare decisions and expenses that could arise as I age?
- Wealth: Is my financial plan flexible enough to support me for 20–30+ years in retirement?
- Lifestyle: How do I want to spend my time in retirement? What would a fulfilling day look like?
- Relationships: Who will I lean on, and how can I support those I love without becoming a burden?
- Wellness and Purpose: What brings me joy, and how will I keep those activities in my life?

Identify Two Immediate Priorities:

- Choose one area from above where you feel strongest and one where you feel least prepared. Start where you have momentum, and plan support where you need it.
- Recognize What Matters Most: Are you more concerned about protecting your loved ones? Securing your lifestyle? Leaving a legacy? Understanding your values will help shape every future decision.
- Jot Down Initial Insights: Capture a few notes—what surprised you, what scared you, and what inspired you. These reflections can serve as conversation starters with your advisor or your family.

True longevity planning starts with an honest, holistic inventory—not of what you have, but of what you value.

2. Create a Personal Longevity Checklist for when you meet with your advisor:

This isn't just about planning for the end—it's about designing a life you want to live, protect, and pass on. Use this checklist to explore four essential areas of your retirement strategy:

◈ *Health Care*

- Review your current healthcare coverage, including Medicare, employer plans, and private insurance.
- Assess your potential extended care or long-term care needs and coverage gaps.
- Explore options for funding care, including insurance products, self-funding, or hybrid solutions.
- Explore preventive and wellness programs that can help reduce future health risks.
- Evaluate local services and caregiving support resources in case health challenges arise.

◈ *Wealth Care*

- Review your income streams in retirement, including Social Security, pensions, and investments.
- Develop a withdrawal strategy that strikes a balance between growth, protection, and longevity.
- Evaluate tax-efficient strategies for legacy planning and asset transfer.
- Revisit your estate plan—beneficiaries, wills, trusts, and power of attorney.
- Consider inflation protection and how unexpected expenses could affect your plan.

◈ *Family Care*

- Define your caregiving preferences—who you'd want involved and how.
- Discuss family meeting strategies—ways to bring loved ones into your plan proactively.
- Plan for multigenerational support, especially if you're part of the sandwich generation.
- Document and share your wishes for aging, care, and medical decisions.
- Clarify roles and expectations early to reduce conflict later.

◈ *Fun Care (Lifestyle Planning)*

- Define what "quality of life" means to you in retirement.
- Plan for travel, hobbies, second careers, or volunteer work.
- Set aside a "joy budget" for the experiences and indulgences that matter most.
- Identify social goals—how you'll stay connected and engaged with others.
- Protect time and resources for the pursuits that bring meaning and fulfillment.

A personalized longevity checklist keeps your focus clear and your goals actionable. It also helps your advisor guide your planning based on what *you* value most, rather than just adhering to the industry standard.

3. Commit to a Timeframe:

Knowledge without action is just potential. To transform your longevity vision into reality, you need forward motion, and that starts with setting a timeline.

Choose a Specific, Meaningful Milestone:

- Don't just say "someday." Mark your calendar. Whether it's by your next birthday, the end of the quarter, or before an upcoming life event, tie your planning to a clear date that motivates you.

Start with a Single, Doable Action:

- Commit to completing the *first step*—perhaps it's booking a one-on-one consultation with your advisor, gathering your insurance and healthcare documents, or setting up a family meeting. Small actions done consistently beat grand intentions postponed indefinitely.

Break Big Goals Into Weekly Wins:

- Create a short list of 2–3 tasks you can complete over the next 30 days. When momentum builds, so does confidence.

Share Your Intentions:

- Tell someone—your spouse, your children, your advisor. Public accountability increases follow-through. Let them know your goal and the date you intend to take that first meaningful step.

Revisit and Reset:

- Life happens. If you miss your deadline, don't abandon the goal. Set a new date, reassess your plan, and keep going. Forward is forward.
- Committing to a timeframe transforms a hope into a decision. It puts urgency behind your intentions—and makes your future a priority, not a someday project.

As the session drew to a close, the room remained quietly energized. Notebooks were filled, action steps were sketched out, and conversations lingered with a sense of shared direction.

Nicole stepped forward, her voice calm but filled with conviction. "What you started tonight isn't meant to be finished in one sitting. This is your launch point—a living, breathing plan that will grow with you. The most important thing is that you've started."

James joined her, glancing around the room at familiar faces and new ones. "We'll be following up, and our team is here to support you every step of the way. This is just the first layer of your roadmap—together, we'll keep building it."

Nicole smiled. "We'll also be sending out a quick feedback survey—your input helps us tailor future Gatherings to what matters most to you and your family."

Attendees began to gather their things, but the energy lingered—less like an ending, more like the first mile of a longer journey.

James offered a final word as people headed out: "Thank you for trusting us to walk this with you. We're honored to help you build the kind of retirement that reflects your values, not just your numbers. Safe travels home—and we'll see you soon."

With that, the Longevity Literacy Gathering came to a close, not as a conclusion, but as a catalyst for further action. A clear step forward in a world that often delays the most important conversations until it's too late.

CHAPTER 16

The Longevity Roadmap Implementation

From Education to Transformation

A month later, the latest Longevity Literacy Gathering brought together the momentum of the previous two sessions. Now, it was time to move from conversation to customization—creating the first draft of each participant's personalized longevity roadmap.

James stepped to the front of the room, his tone steady and purposeful. "It's good to see so many of you again. Our previous gatherings helped you:

- Evaluate your overall longevity needs
- Identify key priorities with the Personal Longevity Checklist
- Commit to an action timeline with your advisor

"Now that we've explored the broader landscape of longevity," he continued, "it's time to take the next step. Tonight is about collaboration—

about turning insight into action, and building a plan that reflects your unique goals, values, and future."

Joining James at the front of the room, Nicole continued, "Let's move beyond planning to implementation. Longevity planning isn't a journey you take alone—it's a shared endeavor built on trusted guidance, strategic partnerships, and continuous support. Our Longevity Literacy Gatherings have underscored an essential truth: knowledge sparks awareness, but action builds security. The next step goes beyond acknowledging the challenges—it's crafting a tailored strategy that ensures you and your family are prepared."

James glanced at Nicole, and in that nod was the truth they'd both recognized: this is more than education—it's transformation. Their firm has evolved into more than just financial advisors; they are **navigators in longevity planning**, guiding clients toward a future of security, care, and fulfillment. This wasn't just about preparing for healthcare costs—it was about living with intention across every dimension of retirement: financial strength, emotional readiness, physical wellness, and enduring family connections. They both recognized how far this initiative had come. Their firm was no longer just focused on managing portfolios—it was leading a movement in **retirement redefinition**. Their clients weren't just looking for rates of return—they were seeking to coordinate wealthcare with healthcare and face longevity with better control over how they'd live the years ahead.

James stepped forward, pointing to the screen.

"Longevity isn't a journey to take alone—it's one built on strategic guidance, shared insights, and proactive planning."

He looked out over the attendees, "We've looked at the big picture—now it's time to break it into action steps. This next phase is about turning insight into impact, with a plan that reflects your values, your lifestyle, and your future goals."

Nicole, "Let's get started. Let's break it down into actionable steps."

James stepped beside the screen, remote in hand, as three simple words appeared:

"Plan. Share. Connect."

"Tonight," he began, "we're introducing three essential strategies that can take your longevity roadmap from concept to reality. These aren't theories—

they're the steps we're seeing successful clients implement across the board."

Nicole chimed in, stepping closer to the audience.

"And before you tune out thinking this is another checklist, let me stop you right there. This isn't about more paperwork or more meetings. It's about clarity—making sure you know where you're going, who's involved, and how to stay on track."

James clicked to the first slide:

1. Partner with a Holistic Advisory Team

James offered some guidance as the attendees read the slides. "This isn't just about investment strategy anymore. It's about a longevity strategy. That means aligning your finances with your health needs, estate goals, business plans, as well as your housing and caregiving preferences. We've built a team of experts—people who specialize in Medicare, Social Security, elder law, business tax law, and selling a business. Even caregiving transitions—so that you don't have to piece this together alone."

Nicole added, her tone conversational, "You might wonder why this matters now. The insights shared tonight are just the foundation. The next step is to leverage experts in crafting a proactive, customized plan that takes into account shifting lifestyle priorities. Think of it like assembling your personal advisory board. You don't need to become an expert in every field—but you should have one in your corner."

2. Bring Your Family into the Conversation

They move to the next slide, Nicole continues, "Now, let's talk about the topic most people avoid when it comes to sharing plans—family."

Nicole makes a funny face, conveying 'you know what I mean.'

Laughter ripples across the room.

"But seriously", she continues, "your plan won't work if it lives in your head or on a flash drive. You've got to communicate it. Not everything, but enough that your loved ones know how to support you—and each other."

James adds, "These conversations don't have to be scary. They just need to be honest. We'll help guide them where appropriate if needed, especially when it comes to defining roles and avoiding confusion during a crisis. We facilitate these discussions, so they happen early—before a crisis forces them. Our team doesn't just plan for your future; we want to help ensure your family is part of that planning process since, honestly, they are part of your future."

3. Build a Longevity Support Network

When the next slide comes up, James says, "The truth is, life changes. The best plans adapt. That's why we're creating a support network you can access not just tonight, but as your life evolves."

Nicole adds, "From one-on-one consultations to Longevity Literacy Gatherings like this one, to curated tools and articles in our resource library—this is just the beginning. **Our firm is a lifelong resource:** The firm's expansion into Longevity Literacy isn't just about one-time sessions—it's about sustained, evolving support. Whether through individual consultations, structured Longevity Literacy Gatherings, or ongoing updates to their Longevity Resource Library, we are committed to ensuring that our clients have access to relevant, evolving guidance every step of the way."

James finishes with, "The most secure clients are the most informed—and the most supported. That's what this network is all about."

Nicole paused, letting the room absorb the weight—and the opportunity.

"Tonight isn't the conclusion—it's the beginning. Now, let's get to work."

◆◆◆

Anchoring Insights with Purpose

Nicole stepped up, "Perhaps the most powerful lesson for tonight is the importance of intentionality. Planning for longevity isn't about fear of the unknown; it's about creating a future aligned with your values and aspirations."

1. Reframe Longevity as Opportunity:

- Instead of viewing longevity as a challenge, see it as an opportunity to shape your legacy, deepen your connections, and embrace life's possibilities with confidence.

2. Take Ownership of Your Roadmap:

- Remember, your longevity plan is uniquely yours. Tailor it to reflect your personal goals, whether they center on financial security, health, or quality of life.

3. Leverage Knowledge to Empower Others:

- Share what you've learned tonight with friends, family, or colleagues who might benefit from the conversation. Longevity literacy grows stronger when it's shared.

◆◆◆

Closing Action Plan

True to her nature as the momentum-maker, Nicole stepped forward to guide the group toward the next steps before wrapping up the gathering.

"Before we end tonight's gathering, let's solidify the energy and focus we've created into a concrete action plan. As you leave, consider these three commitments to guide your next steps:"

1. Define Your Top Priority:

- What's the one thing you'll address this week to advance your longevity plan? Write it down before you go.

2. Book Your First Step:

- Whether it's scheduling a meeting with our team or a specific specialist or setting aside time to review your finances, commit to the next action on your roadmap.

3. Share the Journey:

- Reach out to at least one 'somebody'—a family member, a friend, or even a professional you trust—to share your plan or your commitment. Accountability ensures progress.

Final Words

Nicole offered some final words of encouragement, "Tonight has been about more than asking questions—it's been about helping you find clarity and take control of what's ahead. As you walk away from this gathering, remember: the future isn't something that happens to us—it's something we design with the planning choices we make today. Let this be the moment you take the first step toward a future defined by confidence, resilience, and purpose."

As the last attendee offered their thanks and departed, James and Nicole found themselves once again at their familiar corner in the conference room. This spot—where their ideas and ambitions had taken shape—was now the anchor for something far greater: a successful series of Gatherings that were transforming client awareness and engagement.

"Looks like we're onto something," Nicole said, her voice carrying a mix of pride and relief as the last clients filtered out.

James nodded, the weight of earlier uncertainties lifting, replaced by a quiet conviction.

"Not just something—something transformative, not just transactional."

They weren't just ready to tackle the challenges ahead; they were invigorated by the opportunity to lead, crafting a firm finely and finally tuned to the evolving demands of this generation's retirement and care planning, while positioning it to anticipate and meet the needs of generations yet to come.

CHAPTER 17

Adapting and Evolving: The Power of Client Feedback

The key to a truly impactful and enduring Strategic Growth Plan lies in the ability to listen, adapt, and evolve. It doesn't just rely on broad strokes and preset formulas. A firm's true resilience lies in its ability to remain responsive, deeply attuned to the shifting needs, preferences, and lifestyles of its clientele. This wasn't just about being reactive to market changes; it was about being proactive in understanding the very core of the client experience.

This emphasis on client-driven insights became particularly critical as they developed and refined their Longevity Literacy Gatherings. These sessions were not just educational forums; they were opportunities to engage with multiple generations, uncover shifting priorities, and address unique challenges across different life stages, whether shaped by geographic, cultural, or demographic influences. What worked for one generation didn't necessarily resonate with another. The diverse needs of their multi-generational client base required a flexible, adaptable approach.

As they transitioned from a transactional firm to a holistic planning firm, they discovered that to lead effectively, they had to do more than present ideas—they needed to learn alongside their clients, embracing feedback as a dynamic part of their growth strategy. As they moved forward, James and Nicole knew that to remain relevant and responsive, there would be areas where they needed to adjust their approach, learning not only from their successes but also from their missteps.

With the next steps clearly in sight, it was time to open the door wider—to hear, to adapt, and to grow alongside their clients, ensuring that the road ahead wasn't just about solutions, but about ongoing, meaningful collaboration.

One critical insight gleaned from client feedback was the pressing need to more specifically address a frequently overlooked yet pivotal aspect of retirement planning—complex and rising healthcare costs. Rather than approaching the issue broadly, James and Nicole opted for a more focused strategy, segmenting their clients into three key retirement phases: pre-65 retirees navigating gaps in coverage, the Medicare phase beginning at age 65, and the later-life stage, when healthcare expenses often escalate dramatically.

Their strategy wasn't just well-intentioned; it was anchored in data. The Retirement Confidence Survey, conducted by the Employee Benefit Research Institute (EBRI) and Greenwald & Associates, revealed a striking statistic: 70% of Americans retire before qualifying for Medicare. This highlighted the urgent need to prepare clients for the financial vulnerabilities during this critical transition. For James and Nicole, these weren't just numbers on a report—they represented a responsibility to ensure their clients' futures remained secure during one of life's most unpredictable phases.

◆◆◆

Integrating Client Feedback: Refining the plan

Pre-Medicare

James and Nicole carefully curated a group of clients and prospects who shared a common concern: managing healthcare costs before reaching

Medicare eligibility. It was a topic often overlooked in traditional retirement planning, yet one with profound implications for financial security. By addressing it directly, they aimed to fill a critical gap in their clients' understanding and preparation.

At the Pre-Medicare Literacy Longevity Gathering, Nicole reintroduced a familiar face.

"Some of you will recognize Dan from our Extended Care session," she began with a warm smile. "He helped us make sense of the long-term care landscape—and tonight, he's back to help us tackle another crucial topic: Medicare."

She took a step forward, scanning the room. "More and more, we're hearing from clients who are not only planning their own retirement but are helping their parents navigate this maze. Some of you are already asking the right questions. Others—well, your parents may need your help more than they're letting on. This conversation is just as much for them as it is for you."

Nicole paused to let her words settle before continuing, "Dan's professional expertise in Medicare planning is deep—but what makes his insights so valuable is the personal experience he brings to every conversation. He's helped countless individuals navigate the Pre-Medicare transition with confidence, and tonight, he's here to help you do the same."

With that, Dan stepped forward—ready to guide the room once more, this time through the often-confusing terrain of Medicare, with the same mix of knowledge and empathy that had already earned the group's trust.

On the cusp of retirement himself, he brought a unique blend of credibility and relatability to his presentation. Dan's approach was clear and actionable, offering strategies explicitly tailored for pre-Medicare retirees and emphasizing the importance of early planning.

Dan clicked the remote, bringing up a clear bullet-point slide titled:

"Pre-Medicare Topics We'll Cover Tonight":

- **Medicare Basics:** Eligibility, timing, and the choices between Original Medicare, Advantage Plans, and Supplements

- **Enrollment Windows & Strategy:** When to sign up, enrollment pitfalls to avoid, and optimizing timing based on work and family priorities
- **Cost Considerations:** Premiums, deductibles, co-pays, and out-of-pocket exposure—what to watch for
- **Prescription Drug Coverage:** Stand-alone Part D vs. integrated drug plans in Advantage offerings
- **Coordination with Other Coverage:** How Medicare interacts with employer or retiree benefits, health savings accounts, and COBRA
- **Special Case Scenarios:** Planning for dual eligibility, caregivers, transition risks, or changing health needs

Dan paused, ensuring the audience could absorb each item.

"These aren't buzzwords—they're real decisions people are making right now. And having clarity now can save time, money, and maybe even a few headaches down the road."

Dan stepped forward, clearing his throat as the slide changed to display the first set of options. His tone was calm and conversational.

"So let's talk about your healthcare options before Medicare—and after—with practical, actionable ideas that can ease the transition." He gestured toward the screen.

He explained, *"First up: leveraging a spouse's employer-sponsored plan.* Yes, it may result in slightly higher premiums—but if it works for you, it's a solid and flexible option. Coverage stays intact, continuity is maintained, and enrollment rules are familiar."

Nicole pitched in, nodding. "Especially when one spouse is still working—it keeps things simpler."

Dan clicked to the next bullet.

Continuing, he said, "*Option two: enrolling in a new employer-sponsored plan through part-time work.* Useful for many retirees who choose to stay engaged professionally, but be careful around earnings limits. If you're working part-time and still receiving Social Security, your earnings can reduce your benefits. We urge you to calculate those thresholds *before* committing."

A hand shot up. Dan smiled. "Yes?"

The attendee asked about recent changes to earnings limits. Dan responded with clarity, and the audience relaxed as they realized the guidance was pragmatic rather than theoretical.

◆◆◆

Dan advanced the slide and continued, *"Option three: COBRA.* You can keep your employer's plan post-retirement, but premiums can be steep. Be sure to factor in the entire cost, including retiree costs, insurer fees, and administrative charges. COBRA is a good short-term bridge, but not usually a long-term solution."

Dan paused and smiled before moving on.

"Option four: purchasing private insurance—either through the ACA marketplace or directly. The benefit? Choice. The tradeoff? You'll want help navigating subsidy eligibility, provider networks, and plan design. That's where working with a knowledgeable broker—or us—makes all the difference."

Nicole nodded again, adding, "Tailored options meet your needs—not the other way around."

Finally, Dan clicked on the last bullet:

"Option five: Consider a high-deductible health plan with an HSA**.** This combo offers triple tax advantages—you get tax-deductible contributions, tax-free growth, and tax-free withdrawals for qualified medical expenses. And yes, a high deductible isn't easy—but if you're healthy and disciplined, it can save you significantly over time."

He paused, allowing the group to digest the information.

Then, Dan concluded:

"All of these options can be part of your roadmap. The key? Understand the costs, the timing, and the coordination with your overall longevity plan. That way, you're making confident, informed decisions—not just guessing."

As Dan concluded his detailed and impactful presentation, Nicole stepped in to wrap up. She watched with satisfaction as clients responded with thoughtful, specific questions—a clear sign that the session had resonated deeply.

The interest didn't end with the presentation. Many attendees sought follow-up appointments to explore how these strategies could be tailored to their individual situations. Recognizing the significance of this response, James and Nicole determined that in-person meetings at their office would provide the best platform for these deeper conversations. For attendees who wanted their advisors or family members involved, the newly installed technology in their conference room offered seamless virtual integration, ensuring everyone's voice could be part of the discussion. This thoughtful accommodation underscored their commitment to collaboration and their clients' peace of mind. The strong interest validated not only the importance of addressing healthcare costs but also the effectiveness of their approach. These sessions were becoming indispensable—not just for their clients' financial security, but for the firm's mission to grow as a responsive, forward-thinking practice.

◆◆◆

Exploring Medicare

Building on the momentum from their first session, James and Nicole had carefully selected participants for tonight's focus: entering the Medicare-eligible phase—what Nicole jokingly referred to as the "64-ish" moment—when retirement planning shifts into a critical enrollment stage. They encouraged attendees to invite their adult children or other family members, recognizing that Medicare decisions often span generations and benefit from shared insight.

Behind the scenes, their team had also deepened its capabilities. Knowing that Medicare is state-specific and notoriously complex, they partnered with a respected Field Marketing Organization (FMO)—a vital engine in the Medicare ecosystem. FMOs recruit, train, support, and monitor independent Medicare agents while offering direct access to regionally licensed specialists.

This partnership gave James and Nicole a powerful advantage: they could offer clients not only educational gatherings but a streamlined path to trustworthy, vetted experts. Whether clients needed help enrolling, comparing plans, or evaluating long-term strategies, their FMO partners ensured guidance was available—personalized, local, and compliant.

This approach not only empowered individuals turning 65 but also enriched family discussions around extended care costs, ensuring these milestones were met together and aligned with long-term goals.

Nicole opened the session by welcoming both in-person and virtual attendees with her signature blend of warmth and clarity:

"Good evening, everyone. Tonight's session is about empowerment—arming you with the insights and tools to approach Medicare with confidence. Whether you're planning for yourself or guiding a loved one, our expert is here to help you leave with a clear understanding of your options. Let's dive in."

James followed, his steady demeanor complementing Nicole's energy. "Medicare can be overwhelming, and even a small misstep can have lasting implications. Our goal tonight is simple: to demystify the process and help you align your healthcare choices with your broader financial and retirement plans."

The specialist's presentation was clear and precise, cutting through Medicare's labyrinthine details to address enrollment periods, coverage gaps, and supplemental options. Clients listened carefully, asking thoughtful questions that ranged from the best timing for enrollment to navigating the nuances of Medicare Advantage versus Medicare supplemental insurance. Nicole, always attuned to the room's energy, seamlessly addressed some general inquiries while deferring the more technical ones to the presenter, noting the need for follow-up on more intricate cases, ensuring that no concern went unresolved.

These sessions weren't just a benefit to clients—they also became a goldmine of insights for the firm's blog. The real-time questions and discussions provided authentic, relevant content without the added expense or effort of extensive research—a point that James, always mindful of efficiency, found particularly satisfying. Nicole had teased him relentlessly when the blog was first introduced, playfully reminding him of his initial reluctance. "You were so worried it would 'spread us too thin,'" she had said, grinning as she mimicked his cautious tone. "Turns out, our clients are practically writing it for us."

As the session ended, attendees expressed their gratitude before making their way out. At the same time, the last virtual participant signed off, James and Nicole found themselves back in their conference room, reflecting on the evening's success. For them, the true measure of success wasn't merely about education —it was about equipping clients with the clarity to move forward with confidence. Clients who had once viewed Medicare as an insurmountable maze were now engaged, informed, and, above all, empowered to take the reins of their planning.

◆◆◆

The Later Years: Post-Medicare Challenges and Solutions

Once again, back in their usual spot in the conference room, James and Nicole prepared the content for the upcoming Later-Life Longevity Literacy Gathering, which would focus on the phase where healthcare costs often surge.

"Later-Life Longevity Literacy Gathering," James muttered. "Sounds like a tongue-twister designed by a PhD with a thesaurus addiction."

Smiling, James settled into his chair, then took a sip of coffee.

Laughing, Nicole added her own clever remark! "Later-Life Longevity Literacy Gathering," Nicole repeated. "Sponsored by the League of Alliteration and Complicated Branding."

James was clearly amused.

Nicole placed her steaming mug on the table. But instead of sitting, she walked over to retrieve a heavy bag she'd left on the far side of the room.

"I've been following a speaker who might be perfect for this event," she began, her voice animated as she returned to the table. "What sets her apart is how she weaves her personal story into her presentations. It's not just compelling—it's seamless. She blends years of expertise in the financial industry with deeply relatable narratives."

Placing the bag beside her chair, she continued, "She's specialized in extended and long-term care planning, and her books are widely regarded as go-to resources. They're packed with practical solutions that help families prepare in advance to navigate the complexities of caregiving and the unwanted financial impacts that can accompany it."

"I heard her speak, and her narrative was both compelling and deeply relatable. She detailed her family's journey through the challenges of long-term care, starting with her mother's diagnosis of a debilitating disease. The family's earlier financial and organizational planning became the foundation supporting them through the ordeal of losing their mother. Each of the three sisters had a clearly defined role within the care plan, supported by their mother's long-term care insurance that alleviated financial strain. This foresight allowed them to focus on what truly mattered—spending meaningful, quality time with their mother during her final years, free from the confusion and stress that unprepared families often face. In contrast, when she remarried later in life, she stepped into a family unprepared for the inevitable chaos that came with it, where uncertainty, difficult decisions, and financial strain engulfed all relationships. Bitter arguments erupted when his mother required care, increasing as the level of care increased, leaving the family emotionally bitter and financially stressed. The stark contrast between the two families inspired the speaker to write a series of books on extended and long-term care planning, addressing solutions for a variety of scenarios—whether clients were insurable, non-insurable, underinsured, or seeking alternative approaches."

"Her methodology is as practical as it is powerful," Nicole continued, "and I think she could really resonate with our clients. But what excites me most is her Three-Step Roadmap. It's not just a tool for families; it's a game-changer for advisors, too. This framework brings structure to what is often overwhelming chaos."

James tilted his head, a flicker of curiosity in his expression, intrigued by Nicole's enthusiasm. "Let's hear it. Walk me through the roadmap."

Nicole, ever the natural performer, shifted her stance with deliberate flair, lifting the book slightly to underscore its significance. "This roadmap isn't just a set of abstract ideas—it's a guide that transforms overwhelming what-ifs into manageable action steps. Let me break it down for you so you can see just how practical—and effective—it can be."

With a flourish, Nicole reached into her bag and pulled out copies of all three books, one set for her and one set for James. She picked up the second one. Turning toward James, she pointed to the blue one, a confident smile playing on her lips. "Let's dive into this one, 'How Not To Pull Your Family Apart: A Practical Guide to Caregiving and Financial Stability."

◆◆◆

The Three-Step Roadmap to Care Preparedness

The Care Guide: Empowering Families and Advisors

Nicole flipped through the second book, her finger landing on the section titled *The Care Guide*. Here it is," she said, turning her book to face James and pointing to the page, signaling for him to find the same section in his copy. "The Care Guide is more than just a basic checklist—it's a resource tailored to each family's specific needs. It consolidates everything from birthdates and medical histories to emergency contacts."

James found the section in his copy, quickly skimming the passage, his expression thoughtful as he took in the details. "Makes sense. In a crisis, you'd want all that information at your fingertips. But it's not just medical details, right? I noticed a couple of pages that list content suggestions for questionnaires, worksheets, and it mentioned legal documents and even family traditions being part of it."

"Exactly," Nicole replied, tapping the page for emphasis. "People often assume one legal document covers everything—medical and financial access, power of attorney—but they couldn't be more wrong. This guide encourages families to include various legal documents, along with passwords, heirloom details, and even cherished traditions. It's not just about information, although that is of major importance; it's about preserving what matters most."

James traced his finger along the page, pausing thoughtfully as he considered the implications. "And here," he said, gesturing to a section, "it's about creating a dynamic document—starting with the essentials and layering in detail over time. That's practical. And these 'triggers'—clients can use them to control access, right? For example, one family member might have visibility into legal and medical sections, but not personal reflections or financial specifics?"

"Exactly," Nicole replied, her tone laced with enthusiasm. "That's a game-changer for parents who want to maintain a sense of control or who feel their children aren't quite ready to handle sensitive information yet. They can decide who sees what and when. Plus, this guide isn't something you're expected to complete in one sitting—it's designed to grow and adapt as life unfolds."

James raised an eyebrow. "It evolves?"

"Yes," Nicole continued, her tone sharpening. "Families start with what's immediately needed in an emergency—like medications, allergies, documents, passwords, and key contacts. Then, over time, they can add to it and update it. Maybe they'll include preferences for care or financial instructions. The key is to start now, keep it fluid, and make it a living document."

James tapped his pen thoughtfully against the book. "It's practical and forward-thinking. For clients, especially in the later-life phase, this could make all the difference when the time comes, and they have aging support or care needs. They're not just planning for themselves—they're easing the burden on their families."

"Humm," Nicole murmured, a thought crossing her mind. "As I recall from reading the book, the author suggests that every generation of the family can benefit from starting one. Consider how you already document vaccines and doctor visits for your children. Starting this early could make filling it in over the years much easier. I suspect the author intended this to start before the later-life phase and be instrumental during all dependency events."

"That's the emphasis we want for the gathering—longevity isn't just about living longer. It's about living smarter, planning better, and giving families peace of mind."

The Care Squad: Turning Chaos into Purpose

After a quick break to check for important texts and brew a fresh pot of coffee, they were back at the table, coffee mugs steaming between them, and a small plate of shortbread cookies neatly centered. Nicole reached for her book, flipping through the pages until she found what she was looking for. "Here it is," she said, holding it up briefly before turning it back towards herself.

"Turn to this section," she added, glancing at James. "It starts on page 36." She waited as James flipped through his book, his brow furrowing slightly as he read the bold heading: *The Care Squad: A Framework for Calm in Crisis.*

Nicole waited as he scanned the section, sipping her coffee before she continued. "The author explains it perfectly," she said, her voice steady, inviting him into the concept. She let her finger rest on the diagram. "It's straightforward but profoundly effective. Let me walk you through it."

She smoothed a napkin on the table and uncapped her pen. "The Care Squad," she repeated, her tone thoughtful yet deliberate, "is a tool to turn panic into purpose, confusion into clarity. It's a safety net that every family needs—even if they don't realize it yet. Let me show you."

Row 1: Primary Emergency Contact

"This is your first responder—the person close enough to act immediately when every second counts," Nicole began, sketching the first box at the top of the napkin. "For my dad, it was Maggie, his neighbor. When Dad collapsed, Maggie was at his door in under two minutes. Without hesitation, she called 911. When the dispatcher asked if she could drive him to the emergency room since he was awake but disoriented, Maggie didn't hesitate. She had him in her car and on the way almost immediately. No panic, no delay—just action. Everyone needs a Maggie."

James paused, his coffee hovering near his lips as he processed the example. "That makes sense," he said, his tone reflective, signaling he grasped the gravity of Nicole's words.

Row 2: Back-Up Support

Nicole added two smaller boxes beneath the first. "Next, you need reliable backups. These are the individuals who step in when the primary contact is unavailable. If Maggie hadn't been home, my dad's alert system would have automatically notified the next level of support—my sister and a close friend. They weren't waiting around wondering, 'What should I do?' They knew exactly what to expect because, as a group, we'd mapped it!"

James tapped the napkin lightly with his pen. "But what if emergency responders had been the first on the scene? How would they know to contact Maggie?"

"The author suggests leaving a magnetized note on the refrigerator with the primary and secondary contacts' information—Maggie, in Dad's case, and then me," Nicole explained. "She also recommends carrying a similar note in your wallet. If emergency responders or police arrive, they can easily identify and contact the first responder. Maggie would then activate the next level by calling the person responsible for bringing him personal items or documents to the hospital or emergency room. For my dad, that was me. I have access to his documents and know where his emergency bag is located, as well as which essentials, such as toiletries, a change of clothes, or pajamas, will be needed. Each squad team member knows their specific role, so we can jump into action."

James's expression shifted, his brow lifting slightly as he absorbed the structure of the plan. "That makes it seamless. No scrambling, no overlap—just coordinated effort."

Nicole nodded, satisfied that the concept was resonating. "Exactly. It's about turning chaos into order when it matters most." She continued with her drawing.

Row 3: Roles and Responders

Nicole added a third tier to her napkin diagram, sketching three additional boxes beneath the second level. "This is where the broader team steps in—the people who may not be present in person but can still feel like they play critical roles," she explained, her pen hovering over the freshly drawn boxes, "which, in fact, they do! One person might manage the phone tree, ensuring everyone stays informed. That reduces tension by eliminating confusion and miscommunication. Another could handle logistics remotely, like sorting out hospital bills or coordinating with the insurance company. And someone else would secure the person's house if they were admitted to the hospital or cancel scheduled doctor visits or social engagements." A smooth jazz melody hummed in the background, the warm, mellow tones threading through the quiet hum of conversation. The soft strumming of an acoustic guitar created an ambiance that was both relaxed and engaging, perfect for reflection, yet light enough to encourage conversation.

James leaned back, a pensive look crossing his face as he studied the diagram. His fingers tapped a quiet rhythm against the table, mirroring the steady pulse of the music, as though conducting an unseen orchestra. "You know," he said slowly, his voice carrying the cadence of an idea forming, "this is like a symphony. Every person has a distinct part to play—a defined role. The strings don't clash with the brass because each section has practiced. The conductor doesn't need to bark directions during the performance because the score is already clear."

Nicole tilted her head, listening, a slow smile forming. The analogy fit. The entire conversation, the planning, the structure—it was far more effective than just assembling information. Like a well-rehearsed symphony, the Care Squad was ready when life's unpredictable moments struck—each player knowing their part, stepping in at the right moment without hesitation."

James glanced at Nicole, acknowledging her clever pun! A faint smile tugging at the corners of his mouth, James continues with the metaphor. "When everyone understands their part, there's no hesitation, no missteps. They step in exactly when needed, hit the right note, and everything flows. It's not chaos—it's harmony."

Nicole's eyes lit up with playful admiration. "Exactly!"

Her tone grew more resolute as she tapped the napkin lightly with her pen. "It's about replacing panic with precision. That's the essence of the Care Squad—turning what could be a nightmare into something coordinated and empowering for everyone involved. Emergencies will always be chaotic, but a system like this channels that chaos into constructive action. It's about making sure that the people you trust most aren't left second-guessing when it matters the most. But things don't just stop with extended and long-term care, so there's a fourth layer to the Care Squad."

Row 4: Specific Task Delegators

Nicole sketched four additional boxes at the bottom of the diagram. "This is where the Care Squad becomes an operational powerhouse," she said, her finger tapping the new row with emphasis. "Once the immediate crisis was over and Dad came home, these roles made all the difference—the unsung heroes of recovery!"

She traced the tip of her pen over the first box. "One person handled medical updates—fielding calls and texts so I wasn't trapped repeating the same information on a loop." With a smooth motion, she guided the pen to the next box. "Another managed errands—prescriptions, groceries, whatever was needed." Her pen hovered before gliding forward. "A third ensured the house functioned—meals prepped, laundry done, the little things that keep life moving forward." She looked up, her voice steady.

"Each role was intentional, defined, and essential." She capped her pen with a decisive snap and leaned back, her expression unwavering. "That's the difference, James. It's not about magic or wishful thinking—it's about giving people purpose. When everyone knows their role, there's no spinning, no aimless worrying. Instead, there's action. Focus. Progress."

James considered the diagram in silence. Nicole let the moment stretch and watched as James's gaze traveled over the rows of boxes. He slightly narrowed his gaze, the subtle shift in his expression. It wasn't just passive contemplation—she could tell he was mentally populating the framework, assigning roles and names to each box. Maybe replacing Maggie in the top spot by imagining the reliable neighbor who could be at his parents' door in minutes. Below, a sister takes charge of medical updates, a family friend oversees household logistics, and perhaps a cousin or a volunteer from the church group, which coordinates essential errands for the housebound. The simple diagram wasn't abstract anymore; it was coming alive, filling with real people and practical solutions.

Nicole rose to refresh her coffee, glancing toward James as she reached for the pot. His hand lifted in a small wave, signaling her to skip his refill, his attention fixed on the napkin diagram in front of him. As she walked back to her seat, her mind churned with ideas.

Resettling into her chair, she picked up the book again, her fingers brushing the pages lightly. This framework wasn't just practical; it was catalytic—she could see how well it would fit into their Later-Life Gathering. But an idea began to take shape, igniting a spark of possibility.

"You know," she began, her tone casual but tinged with purpose, "this Care Squad concept has legs beyond just the Later-Life Gathering. What if we created a separate event—something specifically for caregivers and care recipients?"

James looked up, curiosity sharpening his expression. "You mean a dedicated session? Not just a segment in the Later-Life Gathering?"

"Exactly," Nicole replied, leaning forward now, her enthusiasm bubbling over. "Think about it—caregivers are often overwhelmed and isolated, and care recipients frequently feel like burdens. What if we hosted a Longevity Literacy Gathering focused entirely on bridging that gap? Something practical but also deeply empathetic. We could walk them through creating their own Care Squad framework, step by step, and help better recognize the unique challenges they face."

James reached for his iPad to make notes. "That could work," he said slowly. "It would resonate with so many people—families anticipating or already navigating this dynamic in real-time, often without any guidance."

"And it wouldn't just be about emergency preparation," Nicole added. "It could cover communication strategies, financial considerations, and even emotional resilience. It will, of course, have an impact on both the recipients and their retirement plans. We could include breakout discussions—caregivers sharing best practices, care recipients expressing their needs. It could be a transformative experience for everyone involved."

James nodded, his mind already drafting the outline of such a Gathering. "We'd need to structure it carefully, make sure it feels supportive rather than intrusive or overwhelming. But yeah, it's worth exploring. The more tailored we can make these sessions, the more meaningful they'll be. We can involve select staff, so clients have a go-to person- just in case they need a resource link."

Nicole smiled; the moment was charged with shared resolve. "Then let's make it happen. Because caregiving and receiving care aren't just roles—they're relationships. And when they're approached with clarity and coordination, they can be relationships that thrive."

"But let's keep moving. There is another proactive tool," she said, flipping to the next section. "This one is all about avoiding the unintended consequences that come with emergencies by planning ahead. When I was caring for Dad, pulling together the Care Squad was a lifeline. But what kept things steady—what kept me steady—was having a sound plan that fit his health and financial situation. That's where the Care Planning Team comes in." She turned the book toward James again and tapped the page. "Take a look at page 41."

The Care Planning Team (CPT): A Framework for Generational Care

James started scanning the pages. "The Care Squad is already impressive, but this Care Planning Team?" he said, flipping through a couple of pages, "It's like the next evolution—a way to move from reactive problem-solving to proactive, structured planning. It ensures everyone, across multiple generations, is aligned and prepared."

"Exactly," Nicole agreed, her voice gaining momentum. She turned her book toward James, her finger landing on a highlighted quote. "'All journeys have secret destinations of which the traveler is unaware,' by Martin Buber. It's the perfect metaphor for what we're discussing."

She leaned back, allowing the weight of the idea to settle. "The family in this book illustrates the point so well. After an unexpected crisis, they recognized the need for comprehensive, long-term care planning. Balancing immediate care needs with personal obligations and financial realities became their central challenge. Along with the help of advisors, by working together—intentionally—they turned a potential catastrophe into a collaborative effort."

James set the book down, his brow furrowed slightly in thought. "So, it's not just about today's needs—it's about building a roadmap for the years ahead. What's the starting point?"

"The first step," Nicole began, "is assembling the team. But it's not as simple as sending out a family group text. Inclusivity is key—everyone who has a stake in the care process needs to be invited, but with clear expectations. It's not an open-door policy; it's about making sure each person understands the commitment and feels empowered to step back if they can't contribute."

James looked up at her, curiosity evident. "And what if someone opts out?"

"That's perfectly fine," Nicole said firmly. "It's better to have someone voluntarily step back than force participation that leads to resentment. The key is to set boundaries, or "Rules of the Road," so to speak, to ensure everyone knows what's in scope and what's not. This isn't a place for rehashing family drama; it's a space for solving problems."

James let out a small laugh. "I can already picture the arguments brewing."

"And that's why the CPT benefits from a neutral facilitator," Nicole said, smiling. "It works best with an advisor as a trusted third party, as someone to guide the discussion—and mediate if necessary—to keep things productive. Families need clarity and focus; the conflict they can create on their own without any help!"

James let out a low chuckle, rubbing the back of his neck as if shaking off a lingering thought. "That's for sure," he muttered, his amusement fading as he straightened up. His tone grew more serious. "What about the financial side? That's often where families hit roadblocks."

Nicole nodded knowingly. "That's one of the biggest challenges, and the book addresses it head-on in the Rules of the Road. Financial details are not shared with the whole group—they're personal and private. Each member decides who they trust enough to share that information with, whether it's a spouse, a child, or even just their financial advisor."

She paused, her voice softening as she continued. "Older family members often hold back. It's not just about the numbers. Sometimes, it's because their parents didn't share with them, and they're following that example. Other times, it's about fear—fear of losing control, fear of being judged for not planning better, or fear of how their child might judge them if they knew the full picture."

James nodded thoughtfully as Nicole's tone shifted, firm yet empathetic. "Transparency is key—but it's about fostering a space where openness feels safe, not forced. Take the multigenerational family in the book, for example. They approached the topic strategically, sidestepping direct discussions about money at the group level to avoid potential friction. Instead, they focused on exploring options. Each person took responsibility for researching a specific care solution—whether it was home care, assisted living, long-term facilities, or various funding options or strategies."

Nicole placed her elbows on the table, leaning slightly forward as she continued. "What stood out to me was how this method kept emotions in check. Everyone had a role and contributed. Sharing their findings not only informed the decision-making process but also ensured that every family member felt engaged and valued. They even recorded their sessions, so if a member couldn't make the meeting, they could catch up. It diffused tension and allowed the group to prioritize what really mattered: making decisions that were both practical and inclusive, without financial anxieties dominating the conversation."

Nicole remained leaning in; her elbows braced against the table as she cradled her head in her hands. Her fingers pressed lightly against her temples, a posture of contemplation rather than exhaustion. "It's not perfect, but it works because it balances respect for individual boundaries with the need for collaboration. When families encounter roadblocks, it's often because they bypass that delicate equilibrium. Seeing the stark reality of the complexities of Medicare, the Long-Term Services and Support System, and escalating care costs—both current and projected for the future—brings the issue into sharp focus. It's a way to engage in meaningful financial conversations without delving into personal monetary details. And that's where the advisor plays a pivotal role—guiding the discussion, ensuring it stays productive, and helping families navigate the complexities with clarity and purpose."

She paused, flipping to a bookmarked page. "The author even used the storybook family to exhibit creative ways to make the process less daunting and even fun. For example, they began one meeting by accessing an online tool, allowing each participant to estimate their own projected longevity. It led to an insightful discussion about the importance of financial and retirement planning, with each member realizing how longevity impacts every aspect of care."

A grin tugged at James's lips. "That's a clever idea."

"And then there was the time they tried to guess how many counties there are in the United States," Nicole added, a playful edge to her voice.

James raised an eyebrow. "Okay, I'll bite. Two thousand?"

"Not bad," Nicole said, leaning back with a smirk. "But you're still about a thousand counties short."

James exhaled, shaking his head. “Over 3,000? No wonder navigating benefits feels like a bureaucratic scavenger hunt.”

Nicole laughed. “And an additional 140 county equivalents! And, just like Social Security or Medicare, the details matter. Guessing your way through it? Not the best strategy.

In the book, when the person closest to the right number asked, ‘What’s my prize?’ another family member quipped, ‘Not winding up in a care facility that wasn’t your first choice—or worse, one you can’t afford!’”

James laughed, shaking his head in amused agreement. “It’s lighthearted, but it drives home the point. Those small, relatable moments make the bigger picture so much clearer.”

“Exactly,” Nicole said, her tone softening but losing none of its conviction. “The CPT isn’t just about logistics. It’s about creating shared purpose and unity. It ensures families have the tools and the confidence to face challenges together, rather than being torn apart by the weight of unmade decisions.”

James’s expression was reflective as he added, “And that’s what this Caregiving/Care Recipient Gathering is all about; actually, that’s what including longevity and extended care in retirement planning is all about. It’s about more than managing finances or responding to crises—it’s about empowering families to plan in advance. Hence, the plan, with the guidance and expertise they need, reflects who they are and what they want as they age or retire.

CHAPTER 18

The Choice

The Offer

Months had passed since the firm began its transformation, and the changes were unmistakable. The days when everything revolved around reviewing spreadsheets, ROI charts, and retirement plan calculations had evolved into something richer and more impactful. James, who once found solace in the quiet predictability of numbers, now found himself drawn into the deeper, messier realm of human lives and futures. Initially, he had resisted the shift, clinging to the familiar with white-knuckled resolve. However, the results were undeniable: clients expressed a deeper trust in the vision they were building together—discussions that strengthened their confidence in a holistic retirement plan and created a sense of peace, both financially and personally.

Early one evening, with the office cloaked in silence, the kind of silence that presses in when you're alone with your thoughts. James sat at his desk, the pale glow of his monitor casting shadows on his face and the walls. The screen brimmed with projections, yet his focus kept drifting back to Nicole's cryptic hint earlier that day. She had said something big was coming, but had left the details hanging in the air, tantalizingly out of reach. James had a strange feeling that whatever she had to share wasn't just business as usual.

The faint ding of the elevator broke his reverie. Moments later, Nicole appeared in his doorway, her usual air of confidence tinged with something else.

"Well," she began, her tone teasing but her eyes serious, "I'm glad you're sitting down, because what I'm about to show you could knock you off your feet."

James leaned back, crossing his arms as curiosity edged out the fatigue he'd been nursing all day. "Alright, Nicole. What's this about? You've had me on edge all day."

Without a word, she placed the folder on his desk and tapped its cover. The name emblazoned on the cover, instantly recognizable, hit him like a jolt. It wasn't just any name; it was one of the largest National Organizations in the industry, the kind of powerhouse he never expected to hear from.

Nicole stood quietly at his desk as he flipped it open, scanning the contents, his brow alternating between lifting and furrowing as the numbers and proposals began to take shape.

She leaned over and tapped the folder again, her expression a mix of pride and frustration. "It's the third option, James. The one we never really talked about."

Option D: The Temptation of Safety and Reward

James's eyes shot up from the folder to meet hers: a fourth option to grow the business - a merger or acquisition.

Nicole calmly reviewed their journey. We talked about effectively growing the firm. Option A was to leverage AI-driven technology for scalable growth. Smiling broadly, she started off with "My operational foresight led the firm to integrate AI tools long before it became an industry standard. We are now using technologies to enhance everything from client onboarding and communication to predictive planning and customized reporting. We trained everyone on AI-powered platforms to anticipate client needs, automate routine tasks, and deliver highly personalized experiences at scale. Option B was all about building in-house expertise—growing our team, refining our processes, and ensuring the wheels run smoothly. And we nailed it. Option C was all about expanding our network of specialists, bringing in the best minds to handle the parts we couldn't. That's been a game-changer. And now, here comes Option D: Merger or Acquisition."

James's expression was unreadable as she continued, her voice carrying a note of both excitement and caution. "On paper, it's a merger. They want us involved, for now. They'll use our firm as a blueprint for scaling the lifespan, healthspan, wealthspan model we built on a national scale." She paused, holding his gaze. "Then, it becomes an acquisition. They'll phase out our model entirely and fold us into their traditional system. No more health-wealth planning. No more risk of failure."

She exhaled, leaning against the desk, her tone softening but her words sharp. "It's a hell of an offer, James. The money's ridiculous, and the resources—they're promising things we could only dream about. But if we say yes, we lose everything that makes this firm different. And once they're ready to take over, we're out."

James's hand lingered over the open folder; his expression unreadable. "And if we say no?" he asked, his voice steady but quiet.

"We keep building," Nicole replied, straightening. "We prove that this model isn't just a prototype—it's the future. But…we do it without a safety net."

James sat in stunned silence, the weight of the offer settling heavily on his shoulders. It was, by all accounts, a dream deal: financial security, industry recognition, the chance to step away from the risks they'd shouldered during this transformation. And yet, something about it felt... hollow.

Nicole leaned against the desk, her arms crossed. "This is a golden ticket, James. I thought you'd be jumping at this. This is your chance to go back to doing what you're best at-numbers! Just the clean, simple world of investments, wealth management, and retirement planning."

James's voice was quiet but firm when he finally spoke, the weight of his words hanging in the air. "Clean and simple is exactly what we left behind. What we've built—it matters. It's more than just numbers on a page. If we sell, we're giving up the heart of what makes us different."

Nicole sat down, her usual teasing demeanor giving way to a rare, contemplative stillness. She studied him with an intensity that suggested she wasn't just listening to his words, but to the conviction behind them. "I never thought I'd see the day when you'd argue against safety and predictability. You've changed", she said softly, almost as if testing his resolve.

The Crossroads: A Defining Moment for the Firm

"We've both changed." James let out a faint, almost self-deprecating sigh. "Or maybe I've finally realized that real impact doesn't come from playing it safe. Numbers, projections, analysis—they're tools, important tools, but still just tools, not the purpose. What we're doing now—helping people see the full picture of their retirement, including the things they're too afraid to face—that's our purpose."

Nicole's gaze dropped momentarily to the folder lying between them, the offer inside practically burning a hole through the table. When she looked up, her expression was sharper, edged with introspection. "You know," she began, her tone softer now, "you're the one who resisted all this at the start. You insisted that we stick to what we knew, to portfolio analysis and predictability. It was simple, and it worked. And yet here you are," she said, sweeping her hand in a broad arc, as if presenting him to an invisible audience, "championing this."

He met her eyes, unflinching. "Because I've seen what it does, Nicole. I've seen the difference it makes when a widow walks into our office, completely unsure of how to adjust to her new reality. She didn't just ask, 'Do I have enough to live on?' She came to us overwhelmed—beneficiary funds tied up, Social Security adjustments she didn't understand, her Medicare options suddenly shifting, and no clear path forward."

James's voice softened as he continued. "And she didn't come alone. Her children accompanied her, worried about what the future held for their mother. They didn't know where to start, and honestly, neither did she. But I sat with them, listened, and pulled in others, and we worked through every detail—her income, her healthcare and extended care options, her investments, and how to make it all sustainable. We created a plan that not only worked but gave her confidence and her children some peace of mind."

He took a moment, the significance of the memory evident in his expression. "When it was all said and done, she wasn't just relieved. She was grateful. She said, 'Thank you for showing me how to make this part of my life work.' And then her children—who had started the day anxious—asked if we could help them, too. They saw the difference we made for her, and they wanted to be part of what we do. We will see them at the Longevity Literary Gatherings."

James squared his shoulders, his voice steady but impassioned. "That's what we're leaving behind if we merge or sell, Nicole. That's what we lose."

The room grew still again, reflective of the moment. Nicole exhaled sharply as she leaned forward, tapping the edge of the folder with her fingernail. "You're asking me to walk away from a sure thing, James," she said, her voice laced with frustration and determination. "Do you realize what that means for me? Growing this in-house team, building the network of advisors—that's been on my shoulders. Every time we've expanded, every time we've brought in someone new, I'm the one making sure it all runs smoothly. Operations, HR, systems—it's not exactly glamorous, but without it, this whole model falls apart."

She stood up and started to pace, her movements sharp and deliberate, as if each step helped her organize the storm of thoughts swirling in her mind. When she reached the end of the room, she turned on her heels, leveling a sharp gaze at him. "And let's not forget, while I'm doing all that, I'm still bringing in clients. You've brought in your fair share, I'll admit. They come to us because they see how holistic our approach is, how we're doing something better than our competitors. But those clients don't stick around unless the back-end machine works—and that's on me."

Her tone softened, though it didn't completely lose its edge. "So, forgive me if I'm not ready to just toss this substantial sum that would allow me the opportunity to take a year off and travel and relax! This isn't just a business decision. It's years of my life, my health, my reputation, and my work. If we're going to walk away from a golden parachute, we need a damn good reason."

James held her gaze, unwavering. His voice was steady, but beneath it lay something deeper—a quiet conviction that refused to waver. "We do have a reason, Nicole. A damn good one. Because what we've built isn't just about us—it's about the lives we've supported or changed."

He leaned forward slightly, his tone low but resolute. "Think about the woman who came in the other day—a solo ager. She didn't just come to us for a plan; she walked in alone, overwhelmed, unsure of how to step into a future she never expected. She didn't need another spreadsheet. She needed someone to steady her, to help her piece together what her future could look like if she truly understood her options and her plan. And she chose us—trusted us—not because of numbers on a page, but because of the reputation we've built. Credibility. Compassion. Trust. A commitment to standing beside people when they need it most."

James exhaled, the weight of it settling in the space between them. "That's what we're leaving behind if we sell, Nicole. That's what we lose."

Nicole looked away, the intensity of his words hanging between them. She ran her fingers through her hair, her mind racing.

Finally, she let out a long breath. "Alright, alright," she said, her tone quieter now, but no less determined. "If we're going to do this, *we* need a real plan. We proved this lifespan, healthspan, wealthspan model isn't just viable—it's the future," Nicole said, her voice gaining strength as she spoke.

She paused; her gaze unwavering as it locked on James. "But James…" Her tone sharpened, her words cutting through the lingering silence. "You better believe I'm coming up not only with contingencies for every 'what if' scenario but innovative ideas as well. Because this time, the risk and work fall on both of us, not just me."

She straightened, crossing her arms tightly across her chest. "Do you know how many times I've had to carry the fallout? All the late nights scrambling to fix what didn't go as planned? Finding the right internal and external relationships. You, my numbers guy, did the negotiations, but I had to find them. The endless meetings to clean up after decisions you didn't fully support, because you were second-guessing me while I was out there putting my name—and my reputation—on the line? It's been a lot on me, James. Missteps, adjustments, hard conversations with the team."

Her words hung in the air, unflinching and raw, but there was no venom behind them—only the exhaustion of someone who had shouldered more than her share for far too long. James lowered his gaze for a moment, then lifted it again, his expression softening, laced with something that looked like regret.

"You're right," he admitted quietly. "I haven't always had your back the way I should've. I've second-guessed decisions that turned out to be right because I was afraid of what we might lose. But not this time. If we're all in, we're all in. No second-guessing. Not from me—not anymore.

That doesn't mean we won't be smart about AI. A new report shared by Pindrop, a leader in voice authentication and fraud detection technology, reveals a 1,300% surge in deepfake fraud across industries in 2024. According to the report, fraud attempts jumped from an average of one per month to seven per day, while fraud in contact centers reached its highest level in six years."

Nicole studied him for a moment, her expression unreadable, before a faint smile curved her lips. "Good. Because that's the only way this works."

She let the silence linger for a beat, then added with a sly grin, "And just so we're clear—if this all goes south, I'm still the one with the better lines for the memoir."

CHAPTER 19

Managing Growth Challenges and Opportunities

The Departure: Navigating Uncharted Waters

Things had settled down into a predictable, satisfying cadence. The practice was growing in stature and profitability. Staff members seemed happy in their roles, and clients were pleased to recommend the firm to their friends and family.

As the morning's scheduled weekly team briefing/meeting wrapped up, Peter lingered near the door, his posture stiff, his gaze fixed on the floor.

"Peter?" Nicole called, her voice cutting through the hum of colleagues filing out. He flinched slightly but didn't move.

"Is something going on?" she pressed, exchanging a quick nod with James before stepping toward him.

"Uh, can I talk to you both for a minute? Privately?" he asked, shifting uncomfortably.

James and Nicole exchanged a glance before motioning for him to close the door.

Peter ran a hand through his hair, avoiding their eyes. "First, I just want to say how much I appreciate everything you've done for me. The opportunities, the mentorship... I wouldn't be where I am without you.

Nicole's brow furrowed. "What's this about, Peter?"

"I've been thinking about this for a while," Peter continued, his words tumbling out in a rush. "And it's not an easy decision, but... I've decided to leave the firm. I'm starting my own practice." Peter raised his hands defensively. "I'm not going to a competitor! I would never do that to you. I just... I've outgrown this role. I want to try something new, and I need to see if I can build something on my own."

Nicole shook her head, frustration and hurt clear in her voice. "Peter, we've invested so much in you. We've covered your training, paid for your designation and certification, promoted you to our clients, built your reputation alongside the firm's—and now you're walking away without even discussing this with us?"

Peter looked down, his hands fidgeting. "I know. And I'm grateful for everything. I've committed to taking the next step in my career.

Nicole's expression tightened as she stepped closer. "If you'd come to us, we could have talked about it. Maybe we could've worked together to create something new—like a satellite office—where you could have built your own practice with our support, without blindsiding us or disrupting our clients. But springing this on us like this, after everything we've done for and with you, Peter, it's not fair. Not to us, not to the team, and certainly not to the clients."

Peter winced, guilt flashing across his face. "I didn't mean for it to come across like that. I just... I didn't know how to bring it up. I thought this was the cleanest way to move forward."

James's shoulders squared as his frustration grew, his voice sharp. "The cleanest way? For whom? From our perspective, this decision is creating chaos, not just for us, but also for the clients who rely on you and trust you as part of *this* team. You didn't give us a chance to find a path that worked for everyone, and now we're left cleaning up the mess."

Peter's face flushed. "James, I'm not trying to hurt anyone, least of all the clients. I'd never encourage them to leave the firm." Peter raised his hands defensively. "I'm not going to tell clients I'm starting a new practice. I won't solicit anyone, I promise."

James stepped forward; his eyes locked on Peter's. "And how will you respond when they ask where you're going?" He paused, his voice softening slightly but still firm. "Because they *will* ask, Peter. Certainly, you've thought of that. You can't lie to them, so what exactly are you planning to say?"

Peter looked down, his voice barely audible. "I... I guess I'd just tell them... I don't know. Maybe that I'm... exploring opportunities."

James's expression hardened, his frustration evident. "You *guess*? You don't know? Peter, these are *their* plans, their futures. They'll see through vague answers and be left feeling uncertain and anxious. And then some will follow you—not because they want to, but because they're afraid not to. You've built trust with these clients because of your position here. Your departure could lead them to question the stability of the firm, their plans, and even their own futures. And if any of them decide to leave with you, we could face serious consequences. This could affect their accounts, their long-term strategies, and our ability to serve them without disruption.

Nicole exhaled sharply; her arms crossed. "Peter, you are a professional, but the way you have gone about this isn't just unprofessional—it's reckless. If you'd talked to us earlier, we could've helped manage this transition responsibly, but now we're backed into a corner."

Nicole shook her head, her expression a mixture of disappointment and anger, but her voice was steely. "It's not just about the clients either. You've signed non-compete and non-solicitation agreements. If you so much as imply that following you is an option, or they just make that assumption and you aren't clear that it is not an option, it's not just bad faith—it's a breach of contract. And while we've always treated you fairly, don't think for a second that we wouldn't defend the firm and our clients if it came to that."

Peter's eyes darted between them, his defensiveness faltering. "I don't want this to get ugly. I just want to branch out, that's all. I won't take anyone with me. I'll even let them know I'm leaving to pursue something different, but I won't mention my new practice."

James's tone softened slightly but remained firm. "That may not be enough. Even the perception of you taking clients could lead to fallout—for you, for us, and for them. Clients don't like uncertainty, Peter, and this creates a lot of it. That's why we're so careful about transitions like this."

Nicole shook her head; her frustration clearly visible. "You might not think you're hurting anyone, but this decision leaves us scrambling—not just to replace you, but to restore trust with clients and our team. Do you even understand what kind of void this creates?"

Peter sighed deeply, his shoulders sagging. "You're right," he admitted, his voice low. "I didn't think this through the way I should have. I can see now how much I've put at risk—for the firm, for the clients. But I've made my decision, and I've already started making plans to move forward. The cat's out of the bag now."

Nicole uncrossed her arms, her voice calm but tinged with a hint of disappointment. "Peter, you grew alongside this firm. We didn't just invest in your career—we believed in your potential. Every milestone, every promotion, every time we celebrated your success, it wasn't just for you. It was for the team, for the clients, for the legacy we're building together. And now, this?' She shook her head, her voice tightening. 'It's not just a betrayal of trust—it's a rejection of everything we've built together."

Peter shifted uncomfortably, his voice barely audible. "I didn't think it would help. I thought... I don't know. I thought it would just make things harder."

James's voice was clipped as he stepped forward. "Peter, you didn't just make this harder—you blindsided us. And now we're in damage control. This isn't something we can easily fix or delay. You'll need to leave the office now. Come back after hours to clean out your desk, but as of this moment, your access to company systems and client files will be revoked."

Peter's face flushed as he nodded reluctantly. "I understand. I'm sorry it had to end this way."

Nicole's voice was calm but laced with regret. "So are we, Peter. We'll be in touch to finalize the details, but for now, we wish you luck with whatever's next."

Peter hesitated for a moment, then turned and walked out, his footsteps heavy as they echoed down the hall.

James rubbed his forehead and then turned to Nicole. "We have a few hours to figure out how to break this to the team and start damage control. First, I'll cut off his access to everything—company systems, client records, emails, all of it."

"Yes," Nicole said, already jotting notes in her planner. "We need a plan for informing the staff before anyone starts speculating. We should gather them this afternoon and keep the explanation professional but honest."

"And then we need to think about the clients," James added. "We'll need to draft a letter to explain Peter's departure and reassure them about the continuity of their plans."

Nicole tapped her pen against her planner. "Agreed. We also need to deal with his upcoming Longevity Literacy Gatherings. The presentations he was scheduled to lead are only weeks away. We need someone to step in, or we risk losing momentum."

James nodded, his expression grim. "We'll start by redistributing his responsibilities among the team. But we'll need to start looking for a replacement specialist immediately—someone with the right expertise, qualifications, and alignment with our approach."

Nicole sighed heavily, "He's not just leaving a void—he's taking part of our foundation with him."

James and Nicole grabbed some coffee and found their favorite corner of the conference room. Warm coffee aroma filled the air, but without the usual sunset filtering through the blinds. The tension from Peter's departure lingered like a storm cloud.

"This is emotionally harder than I ever would have imagined. Although I never imagined…" she didn't finish the sentence. Nicole stared into her cup. Her voice was quieter than usual, weighed down by the shock of Peter's announcement and the immediate challenge of finding the right specialist to fill Peter's shoes.

James nodded; his hands wrapped around his mug as if grounding himself. "It's not just the clients or the logistics," he said after a pause. "It's the breach of trust. I never saw it coming from Peter."

Nicole exhaled heavily, leaning back in her chair. "Neither did I. I keep thinking about all the years we've worked together, all the conversations about how we built this firm on trust—trust with our clients, but also with our team. And now this? It feels like he threw it all away."

James set his cup down with a quiet clink. "We can't dwell on it too long. We need to focus on what's up next. We'll figure it out, but we need to stay sharp."

Nicole nodded, her gaze steady now. "You're right. We'll start with the team meeting this afternoon. I wonder if he confided in anyone on the team. We need to get ahead of any speculation and lay out a clear plan."

James reached for his iPad. "And we'll draft the client letter tonight. The sooner we address this, the better. Peter might not have thought things through, but we can't afford not to. And once the immediate damage control is underway, we'll need to start tackling the biggest challenge—finding someone to step into Peter's role and take over his responsibilities."

James leaned forward, his voice steady. "This isn't how I wanted today to start, either, but challenges like these remind me why we started this journey in the first place. We've faced setbacks before, Nicole, and we've always come out stronger. Let's channel that into what comes next."

Nicole met his gaze, a flicker of determination returning to her expression. She raised her coffee cup in a silent toast. "To resilience," she said quietly.

James nodded, lifting his mug. "To resilience."

◆◆◆

After Hours: The Search Begins

The conference room was silent except for the low hum of the HVAC system, a stark contrast to the usual hum of brainstorming and camaraderie. James and Nicole sat in their favorite corner, coffee cups steaming between them, but neither reached for the familiar comfort.

James broke the quiet first. "Nicole, finding Peter's replacement isn't just urgent—it's critical. The resource library and interim team efforts can patch the gaps for now, but they won't hold up long. We need someone in-house who's not only qualified but ready to embody what we've built here."

Nicole leaned back, her arms crossed, a mix of frustration and determination etched on her face. "We're not just hiring a specialist, James. We're looking for someone to step into a role that's grown beyond its original scope. Peter wasn't just another advisor—he was part of our identity. Whoever replaces him must truly believe in what we're doing. And that's not something a résumé can tell us."

James nodded, his expression tightening. "That's why we need to act and act fast. We'll cast a wide net—reach out to our network, refine our postings, and vet every candidate like it's our own reputation on the line."

Nicole took a sip of her coffee, the warmth steadying her. "And it is. But you're right—we'll find the right person. They are out there. They have to be."

◆◆◆

Finding Carlos: The Missing Piece

After weeks of interviews that felt more like interrogations, Nicole strode into the conference room one morning, a grin tugging at the corners of her mouth.

"James, stop whatever boring spreadsheet you're working on. I've found him."

James raised an eyebrow, leaning back. "Oh? And who is this mythical unicorn?"

Nicole set her coffee down with a flourish. "Carlos Velasquez. You've heard his name before—young but steady, impeccable credentials. But that's just the start. During his interview, when I mentioned the resource library and Longevity Literacy Gatherings, his face lit up like a kid in a candy store."

James's skepticism softened slightly. "Impressive. But enthusiasm alone doesn't make a fit."

"That's the thing," Nicole shot back, her voice brimming with confidence. "He's sharp, thoughtful, and his references might as well be love letters. They couldn't stop raving about his compassion and integrity. He gets what we're doing, James. And more than that, he wants to build on it."

James met her eyes, a spark of curiosity lighting his eyes. "Alright. Let's bring him back for a second round. If he's half as good as you say, I'll eat my skepticism."

Nicole grinned, raising her mug like a victory flag. " I hope you're hungry, James—because you're about to chow down on a five-course meal of 'I told you so.'"

◆◆◆

A New Beginning

They hadn't expected to fill the role quickly—not after losing such a key team member. But then Carlos walked into the second interview and spoke not just about planning or projections, but about *possibility*. He didn't posture or pitch; he listened. And when he spoke, his words didn't just address the work. They addressed the *why* behind it.

James was intrigued. Nicole was all but lit up.

Carlos had a quiet intensity—the kind that didn't need to prove himself because it was always watching, always learning. He discussed planning in a way that some people do architecture: not just what it looks like, but what it makes possible.

And when the conversation turned to AI, Carlos didn't flinch. He leaned in.

"You know," he said, "people keep asking if AI will take over our work. Wrong question. The real question is: will we keep up with the pace of its development? Will we use it like a glorified Q&A machine—or will we train it to think with us?"

James raised an eyebrow. "You think it's possible?"

Carlos smiled, not arrogantly, but with the confidence of someone who had already glimpsed the next chapter. "It's not just possible. It's inevitable. AI isn't here to replace planning. It's here to elevate it. The firms that win will be the ones who use it not to shortcut empathy, but to scale it. Not to guess—but to anticipate. The best advisors will be the ones who don't just work *with* AI, but teach it how to work for the human experience."

Nicole glanced at James, and for the first time, he didn't look wary.

He looked ready.

The Decision to Hire Carlos

They lingered in the quiet conference room after Carlos left—just the two of them, the air still charged like ozone after lightning. It was time for one of their classic "coffee in the conference room" meetings. But this wasn't just a debrief. This was a threshold.

Would Carlos—and everything he carried with him, from AI dashboards to algorithmic insight—be a new foundation for the firm?

Or a beautiful distraction?

Nicole broke the silence first. "This is what leadership in retirement looks like now, isn't it? Not just planning, but building the capacity to adapt. Organically. Externally. And now, operationally.

James nodded slowly, the words settling into the space between them. They'd already expanded their services. Deepened client conversations. Evolved from managing wealth to guiding lives. But Carlos represented something else. Not just talent, but trajectory.

"The game is afoot!" James said, doing his best Sherlock Holmes impression. He leaned back in his chair, half-smirking. "Only this time, it's not Moriarty we're chasing—it's an expanded definition of retirement leadership. It's not about what you already know. It's about what you're willing to unlearn. Who you're willing to trust. And how fast you're willing to adapt."

He tapped the table for emphasis. "Carlos doesn't just talk about AI like it's some shiny gadget. He talks about it like a shift in responsibility. Like a call to level up, not check out."

Nicole, without missing a beat, raised her mug high like a toast. "Hope you're hungry, James—because you're about to chow down that five-course meal of 'I told you so.'"

James chuckled, shaking his head. But behind the laugh, there was something else—respect, and maybe just a little awe. The game was afoot, and to his surprise, he was ready to play.

Finally, he leaned back in his chair. "So, what do we call it? This... thing he's going to lead?"

Nicole smiled, walked to the whiteboard, and wrote in bold letters:

Behavioral Intelligence & Client Experience

She turned back to him. "Not just a department. A declaration."

James read the words, then met her gaze. "It's a mouthful."

"It's the future."

Nicole picked up her coffee, smiling at the steam. "Organic growth got us here. Strategic partnerships are expanding our reach. But this?" She nodded toward the empty chair Carlos had occupied. "This is our edge."

James fell silent, the gears turning. For all his caution, even he couldn't deny the way Carlos had handled their questions—with clarity, with context, and without ego.

He gave a small, reluctant chuckle. "Alright," he said. "Let's make him an offer."

Nicole didn't say anything for a beat. She gestured toward the empty chair Carlos had filled. Then, softly: "We need this."

James looked back at the board. "Carlos isn't just a hire," he murmured. "He's a signal. A shift."

He stood, the words lingering in the space between them.

"It's not about whether the machines are coming."

Nicole nodded, finishing the thought with him.

"They already have, and we have embraced some basic ones."

He looked at her. "Now the only question is—who leads with them?"

◆◆◆

A New Catalyst: From Familiar to Future

When Carlos accepted their offer, the team rallied behind him. Clients noticed the change immediately. Carlos infused the Longevity Literacy Gatherings with fresh ideas and an energy that reinvigorated the entire firm. The resource library, once a concept, became a dynamic hub under his stewardship.

James and Nicole found themselves reflecting one evening, coffee cups once again warming their hands. "You know," James began, "maybe Peter's departure wasn't just a loss. It was a challenge—and an opportunity. Carlos isn't just filling Peter's shoes. He's showing us a different side of what could be."

Nicole nodded, her gaze steady. "Sometimes growth means letting go of what's comfortable. We thought Peter was indispensable, but now I see—it was time for something new. And Carlos? He's the future."

And just like that, the firm wasn't just evolving—it was re-architecting its future, one bold decision at a time.

CHAPTER 20

Strategic Growth Playbook

Building Bridges to the Future: Igniting the Next Spark

In preparation for their next quarterly review, Nicole strolled into James's office, her determined gaze paired with an unmistakable energy. The firm was flourishing—its commitment to adaptability and client feedback had driven steady growth. Yet, true to her nature, Nicole wasn't content to rest on their laurels. James, sensing another of her bold ideas, leaned back in his chair, arms crossed—a posture she knew all too well. It was his *"what are you up to now"* stance. She met it with a teasing grin before he sighed and leaned forward, bracing himself with his hands on the desk. "Alright, let's hear it."

Nicole couldn't suppress her excitement as she tapped out a playful drumroll on the desk. "Big idea incoming! The 'Library,'" she began, "has been a game-changer. Clients rave about it. So… let's level it up! Imagine this: a blog, a Q&A forum, guest specialists sharing insights, and a 'News & Views' section tackling pressing questions and updates that matter to our clients."

James raised a skeptical brow. "A blog? A Q&A forum? Isn't that a bit… ambitious, considering everything else we're juggling?"

Nicole nodded, ready for the pushback. "Maybe. But think about it—clients don't just want sporadic meetings. They crave ongoing insights. A platform like this builds trust and solidifies our role as more than simple advisors—we're holistic guides."

He let out a thoughtful "Hmm," his tone cautious but intrigued. "Alright, but how do we pull this off without overwhelming the team? We've found a good rhythm, and I'd hate to upset it."

Nicole's eyes were bright with conviction. "Remember what Dr. Maureen said at the last Longevity Literacy Gathering? 'Adaptation isn't about abandoning your foundation; it's about building bridges from where you are to where you want to go.' That's what this is, James. The Library gave us the foundation—but this next step? It's the bridge. Not every client connects the same way. Some want data. Some want stories. Some need to hear it from a peer or read it late at night on their own. We don't always know which insight will land, but this expansion lets us meet them wherever they are—and help them move forward."

◆◆◆

James nodded slowly, his practical side finally giving way. "Okay, I see the merit. But we measure everything—engagement, workload, impact. If it pulls us away from the core mission, we reassess."

Nicole grinned, her enthusiasm infectious. "Done. I knew you'd come around. This will elevate everything we've built."

She raised her hands, palms open, like presenting a blueprint drawn in the air. "This isn't just a tool, James—it's a connection. It allows clients to access what they need, when they need it, and brings families together. Whether it's a young client wanting guidance about saving now that she has her first job or a grandchild joining a caregiving session, The Library will offer answers, resources, and support. And it's our legacy. This ensures that what we've built doesn't just survive—it grows and evolves for generations."

James leaned back in his chair, the gears turning. "I get the vision. But the execution... that's the part that keeps me up at night."

Nicole lowered herself into the chair opposite James, her tone even but confident. "That's where everything comes together—AI, our people, trusted partners, and the insights from our data. Basic AI handles the operational noise—automated scheduling, client follow-ups, email sequences—freeing our team to stay fully present in the moments that matter. Our advisors and specialists bring real, human expertise. And when we need outside guidance—healthcare pros, estate experts, caregiving advisors—we lean on our vetted external network. Add in our data dashboards to track what's working and what isn't, and you've got infrastructure that doesn't just support the vision—it keeps it going." She paused, then added, "It doesn't replace our judgment. It enhances it. And let's be honest—soon enough, it might start questioning our decisions before we even think to question them ourselves. So far, every time we move forward with our plan- growing and evolving with the needs of clients and our industry- it's been surprisingly… well, swell."

James raised an eyebrow. "'Swell?'" he echoed, amused.

Nicole laughed, lifting her hands in playful surrender. Then, after a beat, as she stood up, preparing to leave his office, her expression softened into something more thoughtful. "So, we don't just build a Library—we build one that can breathe. One that listens. One that learns."

Stopping in the office doorway, Nicole turned back around, her voice softened, "Exactly. And that's how it becomes a living legacy without becoming a burdensome workload."

Legacy in Action

Months later, the firm had seamlessly integrated these elements. The blog, Q&A forum, and expert guest features became dynamic extensions of The Library, enriching client experiences and cementing the firm's reputation as a trailblazer in credible, holistic retirement planning.

Sitting in their favorite corner of the conference room after a successful event, James swirled his coffee thoughtfully. "Funny, isn't it? The things I've been most hesitant about often became the breakthroughs we needed."

Nicole smiled, lifting her mug. "Here's to the next idea—and to never getting too comfortable."

Beyond the Numbers

"We're not just planning retirement anymore," Nicole had once said during a presentation. "We're planning for life and longevity—with all its twists and turns."

For James, the numbers guy, this evolution was transformative. Mentoring younger advisors became his passion, helping them see beyond spreadsheets to the human stories they supported. The patience and precision he once reserved for financial analysis now guided a new generation of planners.

"The more we share," he told Nicole, "the sharper we stay. Mentoring isn't about teaching—it's about growing alongside them."

Nicole had teased him then, raising her cup in mock toast. "To the reluctant leader who turned out to be a born mentor!"

The Journey Continues

As James and Nicole sat in reflective silence in their usual meeting spot, steaming coffee in hand, they knew the firm's journey was far from over. It had grown beyond numbers into something deeply human—a commitment to navigate life's uncertainties that come with longer lives with compassion and strategy.

Outside, the city pulsed with the steady rhythm of progress—its skyline a testament to visionaries who dared to evolve. Inside, James and Nicole had built something just as enduring—not on steel and glass, but on trust, credibility, and an unwavering commitment to transforming lives. What had once been a firm focused on transactions had become a movement—one rooted in purpose, passion, and the belief that real planning isn't just about numbers; it's about building a future worth living.

CHAPTER 21

Final Reflection

Retirement Leadership Revisited

They began with a single truth: planning today requires more than just managing investments. It requires wisdom, empathy, and adaptability. Along the way, James and Nicole discovered four transformative ways to grow their practice and stay truly relevant in this new world of holistic planning:

1. Organic Growth: Build from Within

Nicole led the charge—earning her RSSA credential, launching the SSRP team, and proving that deepening their expertise in-house was not only possible but also powerful. They didn't wait for external validation. They cultivated it, quietly and deliberately.

2. Strategic Partnerships: Expand the Firm's Ecosystem

They recognized their limits and embraced collaboration. By inviting trusted specialists and Field Marketing Organizations—experts in healthcare, long-term care, and Medicare and Medicare supplemental products—to join their project teams, they strengthened their ability to serve clients without overextending themselves.

3. AI and Tech Enablement: Scale Empathy Through Intelligence

Technology didn't replace them—it amplified them. AI freed them from routine tasks, enabled proactive care, and helped them ask the right questions—at the right time—to uncover what clients didn't yet know they needed.

4. ML&A (Mergers, Licensing & Acquisitions)

When presented with a tempting merger offer, they paused—not out of fear, but out of clarity. They chose to protect their identity and build responsibly. And while the opportunity remains, their commitment is clear: stay true or find another path.

◆◆◆

A Journey Built on Purpose

What began as a debate over spreadsheets grew into a legacy of stewardship. Together, they moved from certainty to care, from transactions to trust, and from fear-bound retreat to courageous leadership. They learned that balance sheets aren't lifelines—it's the families, relationships, and futures that give their work purpose.

"Not Just Financial Advisors. Legacy Builders."

That's the promise they now deliver:

- A practice where every question—spoken or not—is heard
- Expertise that reaches beyond investments into the complexities of life

- Technology that supports empathy, not replaces it
- A future built together—not handed off or folded

Their journey isn't a story of dramatic reinvention—it's one of enduring evolution. By choosing not just to keep up but to lead with foresight and flexibility, James and Nicole have set a new standard, not only in their firm but also for advisors and advisory firms that want to thrive.

◆◆◆

The Next Chapter Starts with YOU

Your firm doesn't have to reinvent itself in a day. But if you're ready to grow—not just survive—these four pillars offer a proven roadmap:

1. Cultivate internal expertise
2. Partner with trusted specialists
3. Leverage technology for empathy
4. Evaluate growth opportunities without losing your soul

Because at the end of the day, clients don't just invest in portfolios—they invest in people they trust to build the lives they envision. And that's what makes all the difference.

The future of financial advising isn't just about sharper tools or better models—it's about leadership. Real, human, values-driven leadership.

As James and Nicole's journey shows, navigating the evolving world of holistic planning requires more than simply staying informed. It requires transformation—both personal and professional, as well as firm-wide. Clients aren't just looking for portfolio performance. They want clarity, connection, and confidence in the people guiding their financial futures.

For firms ready to thrive—not just survive—in this new environment, growth must come from four deliberate areas:

1. Client-Centered Communication

Modern clients expect more than quarterly statements. They want proactive, transparent dialogue. That means using technology to stay connected, but also humanizing every touchpoint through tone, timing, and a deep understanding of life transitions.

2. Intergenerational Relationship Building

The Great Wealth Transfer is already underway. Firms must deepen relationships across generations, understanding each family's dynamics, preferences, and values. Retention in the coming decades depends not just on asset performance, but on emotional and relational continuity.

3. Holistic Service Expansion

Retirement isn't just about dollars and dates anymore. Today's clients want help planning for health costs, caregiving, purpose, and lifestyle. That means firms need to broaden their advisory scope through in-house expertise, trusted partnerships, and tools that address real-life needs beyond the spreadsheet.

4. Advisor and Team Development

The future is collaborative. Firms that thrive will be the ones who invest in developing their advisors, not just technically, but emotionally and strategically. This includes mentoring, AI literacy, and succession planning that fosters a resilient internal culture capable of adapting to evolving client demands.

And now, how will you write your next chapter?

Will you embrace the future, adapt, and lead with purpose—or will you be left behind, watching as the industry moves forward without you?

The next move is yours.

EPILOGUE

Leading Forward

Retirement is no longer a finish line.
It's a pivot point—a handoff between generations, between values, between how we live and how we lead.

In this new era, leadership isn't about having all the answers.
It's about asking better questions.
Creating space for smarter solutions.
Prioritizing connection, adaptability, and long-term relevance.

Throughout this book, you've explored four essential strategies to lead in the new retirement era:

- Grow organically— mentor from within and cultivate the next generation of leadership.
- Grow externally—build partnerships, plan succession, and engage across generations.

- Grow intelligently—leverage AI to challenge and refine human judgment.
- Grow strategically—make bold decisions that align with vision, values, and sustainable scale.

Today's clients span three, sometimes four, generations. Leadership must stretch beyond portfolios and projections to embrace the full spectrum of human life—its complexity, fragility, and capacity for reinvention.

Here's the truth:
AI won't replace your judgment.
But it will test it.
And soon, it may question your choices before you do.

The future belongs to those who lead decisively, adapt relentlessly, and harness intelligence—both artificial and human.

Because in this new retirement era, success won't go to those who move fastest—but to those who see furthest.
And act with purpose.

That's the pivot.
That's the promise.

The future won't just be digital.
It will be deeply personal—shaped by those with the vision to lead differently.

The leaders of tomorrow won't just adapt to change—they'll define it.

About The Author

Carroll Golden is redefining what it means to build wealth—one intentional conversation at a time.

With a powerful foundation in financial services—spanning top-tier advisor networks and leadership roles across the industry—Carroll brings a grounded, strategic lens to planning that goes beyond numbers.

As an award-winning author and sought-after speaker, her work bridges the personal and professional realms, encompassing legacy, caregiving, connection, and financial clarity.

Her message, *"How Do You Define Rich? Let's Build a Plan That Matches It,"* challenges individuals and financial professionals alike to rethink success—not just in terms of dollars, but also in terms of health, harmony, and impact.

She's here to inspire alignment—and deliver tools that help protect what matters most.

Check out the link below for even more by Carroll Golden:

Made in the USA
Studio City, CA
November, 2025

www.ingramcontent.com/pod-product-compliance
Lightning Source LLC
Chambersburg PA
CBHW050526240926
51846CB00003B/708